WHAT IS
SIX SIGMA
PROCESS
MANAGEMENT?

WHAT IS
SIX SIGMA
PROCESS
MANAGEMENT?

ROWLAND HAYLER
MICHAEL NICHOLS

McGraw-Hill

New York Chicago San Francisco Lisbon
London Madrid Mexico City Milan New Delhi
San Juan Seoul Singapore Sydney Toronto

The *McGraw·Hill* Companies

1 2 3 4 5 6 7 8 9 0 FGR/FGR 0 9 8 7 6 5

ISBN 0-07-145341-5

This publication is designed to provide accurate and authoritative information in regard to the subject matter covered. It is sold with the understanding that neither the author nor the publisher is engaged in rendering legal, accounting, or other professional service. If legal advice or other expert assistance is required, the services of a competent professional person should be sought.
—*From a Declaration of Principles jointly adopted by Committee of the American Bar Association and a Committee of Publishers.*

McGraw-Hill books are available at special quantity discounts to use as premiums and sales promotions, or for use in corporate training programs. For more information, please write to the Director of Special Sales, McGraw-Hill Professional, Two Penn Plaza, New York, NY 10121-2298. Or contact your local bookstore.

To my dearest Lizzie, Will, and Em.

R. H.

I have been honored to have many mentors and teachers in my career, more than can be mentioned here. I would like to explicitly call out Dr. Ernest Nichols, Robert C Cobb, Michael D Jones, all of my friends and colleagues at Fed Ex and ASQ, and of course Vinnie Bimboombatts!

M. N.

CONTENTS

FOREWORD

Many companies are working hard to improve the structures for change in their operations. The handsome returns that have been documented through Lean, Reengineering, Six Sigma, and related initiatives show that a focus on customers and processes can really pay off. Business change *can* be improved.

But these evolving change structures are still shaky. Using better problem-solving or business redesign methods is okay *some* of the time, but not all the time. Working cross-functionally is a good concept, but still rarely comes naturally for most organizations.

In other words, the *foundation* needed to support and really sustain new improvement methods is often weak or missing. To understand customers, instill management-by-fact, align and streamline operations, you can't just call it a "project." It has to become a way of life.

Fortunately, we're seeing more and more companies starting to understand that the tools and techniques of Six Sigma are a starting point for learning how to manage smarter. And the best approach to that smarter management is what Rowland Hayler and Mike Nichols explain to us in this book.

Six Sigma Process Management creates the foundational *management* skills and practices that can help a company change the right things, and change them the right way. These pages provide a simple and usable guide to why and how Six Sigma Process Management can solidify and magnify the impact of your business's change efforts.

As you read this book, you'll be reminded that process management is *not* easy (that's why the structures for change are so often built without the foundation). But consider the example of one of our clients, a large and complex titan of the high-tech industry.

By investing meaningful time and effort into one of its critical core processes, it has created a pocket of "culture change." The contrast is striking: People engaged in this "pilot" process (who come from various functions—after all, this is *process* management) are seen by their peers as really understanding their operations. The projects being launched to drive improvement are well defined and move quickly to results. They are able to engage with *other* processes to work on even larger business opportunities.

This company has gotten the message. Using Six Sigma based approaches to achieve process management, so appealing in theory, actually pays off in *practice*. I hope you will use the guidance Rowland and Mike provide to help put *Six Sigma Process Management* in practice for your organization.

Pete Pande
President, Pivotal Resources, Inc.
Walnut Creek, California

ACKNOWLEDGMENTS

Our warmest thanks and appreciation go to the many people who have provided us with support and encouragement throughout the writing of this book. In particular, we would like to thank those companies and individual contributors who have provided content, materials, comments and ideas: James Bossert—Bank of America; Sue Brown, Roland Cavanagh, Dr. Roger Cliffe—Vodafone; Grace Duffy, Ann Grace—International TechneGroup Incorporated; David House—American Express; Liz Keim, Andy Liddle, Steve Moss—Reuters; Ian Palliser, Pete Pande—Pivotal Resources; Roberto Saco—American Express; Rob Smyser—MIT Information Services & Technology; Dodd Starbird, and Dr. Jack West.

Over time we have seen real value delivered from the business principles, methodologies, and tools presented here and are honored to be able to share what we have learned from others.

INTRODUCTION

Over the last few years, we have often questioned whether yet another book on business process improvement is truly needed. After all, it appears that new books on the subject are published almost every week!

Nevertheless, as we surveyed the increasingly rich array of publications on the subject, we began to realize that we have several business process leadership experiences, observations, and ideas that might be of interest and value to others.

Consequently, the purpose of this book is to offer people who have responsibility for driving business process improvement, or who are engaged in such efforts—from large-scale transformational change to small-scale incremental changes—with what we hope are some refreshing new insights and perspectives on how Six Sigma Process Management can be used to achieve *business process leadership*.

In considering how best to organize our thinking, we felt that it would be simplest to communicate our ideas in relation to a number of topics that seem to be commonly raised by people working on business process improvement efforts today:

- In Chapter 1, we define Six Sigma Process Management and explain why it's important. We also describe how it can help your organization achieve improved *process maturity* and operational performance;

- In Chapter 2, we introduce the change leadership requirements that we believe are crucial to successfully implement a Six Sigma Process Management approach;

- In Chapter 3, we offer a step-by-step methodology for implementing a *process management system* within the context of the Lean Six Sigma DMAIC framework. We also outline the key tools required to establish the Six Sigma Process Management system;

- In Chapter 4, we focus on the Six Sigma Process Management requirements that we believe are crucial for successfully managing your *end-to-end processes* on an ongoing basis. These include practical tips and advice for *Process Owners* and others responsible for effective *Process Governance*;

- In Chapter 5, our final chapter, we explore the future of process management and outline the key characteristics of a *"future-state"* organization that has successfully embedded Six Sigma Process Management into its business operations.

As we've written this book, one of the challenges that we've continually been aware of and have wrestled with—along with, we're sure, many other authors writing on technical subjects—is the fact that we essentially have to lay out our ideas in a linear way.

The concern we have with such an approach is that you could perceive our ideas and suggestions for establishing Six Sigma Process Management as a very linear process. This is absolutely not the case!

We have been particularly aware of this issue as we have written Chapter 3, because this probably contains the most technical information in the book.

While there is a logical sequencing of some of the crucial components for establishing Six Sigma Process Management—similarly, a number of the required components can be established concurrently. For example, we suspect that recent actions your company might have taken in order to achieve Y2K and Sarbanes-Oxley compliance have already provided the focus required to better understand your company's core processes. So, if this is the case, your organization already has a *"key component of the Six Sigma Process Management puzzle"* in place!

We also recognize that a high degree of *variation* currently exists in terms of organizations' Six Sigma *process management maturity* and their readiness *and* ability to take the next steps on their process management journeys.

Some organizations might already have completed many Lean Six Sigma projects and increasingly understand the value of using *end-to-end process management* approaches to identify their next waves of projects. Others might be just starting to consider taking a Lean Six Sigma approach to achieve improved performance and are trying to figure out how to identify those all-important, first projects. Others are some place in between.

In recognition of the varying levels of maturity that we have observed—working with numerous clients across many geographies and industries—we have tried to communicate our Six Sigma Process Management ideas with two key principles in mind:

1. We have intentionally constructed this book in a modular way so that you can easily find the specific topics and components that interest you at any given point in time—somewhat like a reference book.

2. We have tried to refrain from being prescriptive in how things need to be done. Our focus is to identify what typically needs to be

addressed and, based on our experience, offer you practical ideas and suggestions on how you might address these challenges within your own organization.

Our intent throughout is to help *you* address the challenges that *you* need to overcome in order to successfully realize the value that a higher level of Six Sigma Process Management maturity will create for the most important company in the world—*your* company!

We hope that you find the ideas contained in this book interesting, helpful, and provocative. We wish you well on your Six Sigma Process Management journey.

WHAT IS
SIX SIGMA
PROCESS
MANAGEMENT?

CHAPTER 1

DEFINING SIX SIGMA PROCESS MANAGEMENT

Perhaps a good place to start is to answer some initial questions that we suspect you might have. In this opening chapter, we will:

1. Define what we mean by the term Six Sigma Process Management and introduce other key definitions that you will find helpful;

2. Explain why we believe Six Sigma Process Management is crucial for current and future business success;

3. Describe how Six Sigma Process Management fits with today's business improvement landscape.

WHAT IS SIX SIGMA PROCESS MANAGEMENT?

Quite simply, we think of Six Sigma Process Management as the *system of management* that enables *process leaders and participants* to, at any point in time, answer the following *critical questions* about their business:

1. What's important to our customers and other key stakeholders?

2. Are our processes fully addressing customers' requirements and those of other key stakeholders?

3. What projects should we be working on, and in what priority order?

4. How do we know that our improvement efforts are creating tangible and sustainable value?

1

WHAT IS THE SIX SIGMA PROCESS MANAGEMENT METHODOLOGY?

The Six Sigma Process Management methodology is a practical approach that focuses the tools and rigor of Lean Six Sigma on your critical processes in order to help you identify the most strategic and customer-focused opportunities for Lean Six Sigma projects in your organization.

In adopting the term "Six Sigma Process Management," we recognize that there might be some people who will be asking "What about Lean? What about Kaizen? What about XYZ?" These are reasonable questions to raise, and before we go any further, let's address them.

In doing so, let's step back for a minute and consider the "big picture." What is it that most companies are continually trying to achieve? At its simplest, we believe it's to:

- Create compelling new products and service offerings;
- Provide service delivery as defined by customers;
- Generate attractive returns for shareholders;
- Be the best place to work for employees;
- Operate mutually value-creating partnerships with third-party suppliers.

Is it possible that any of these constituencies—customers, shareholders, employees or suppliers—care about the "name" or "label" that a company chooses to use to describe their approach to help achieve these objectives? Well, perhaps—but in the grand scheme of things—more likely not! In fact, let's take this line of questioning further for a moment.

Ask yourself this question: As a consumer, do I make "buying" decisions based upon the value proposition (a function of both *"quality"* and *"price"*) of a company's products and services—or do I make "buying" decisions because I know that company A is using Lean, Six Sigma, or some other approach to business improvement, but Company B isn't?

We haven't met any consumers who make buying decisions based on a company's stated business improvement strategy or approach, but we've met lots who make buying decisions on the value (*quality* and *price*) the company offers. *And* as Lean and Six Sigma have shown, they can be highly successful methods for increasing the *effectiveness*[1] and *efficiency*[2] of a company, thereby enabling it to offer compelling value propositions.

Now, at the risk of contradicting ourselves, we do recognize that these *"labels"* have a role in helping organizations energize, focus, and mobilize their improvement efforts. However, the important thing is not to get "hung-up" on these labels, but to stay focused on what it is we're continually trying to achieve.

So, how did we settle on the name—Six Sigma Process Management? We believe this is the most appropriate name for the approach to business process leadership we are proposing because we see a direct lineage with existing and widely used Six Sigma methods, tools, and techniques.

In fact, and this is an extremely important point to note, it's highly likely that your Six Sigma Process Management efforts will identify project opportunities that will be best executed using a number of different improvement, design, and redesign approaches—such as Lean, Kanban, Kaizen, WorkOut, Six Sigma Design, and Redesign. So, although the "label" we've chosen to use is *"Six Sigma Process Management,"* it's important to remember that the intent of this approach is to help you identify the most important business improvement opportunities for your business. The methods, tools, and techniques you subsequently use to execute these improvement opportunities will need to be assessed on a situational basis depending on the scale, scope, and complexity of each opportunity. It's unlikely that Six Sigma methods, tools, and techniques will offer the best approach in all cases! To suggest otherwise is a bit like a doctor prescribing antibiotics in the hope that they will treat every ailment!

Many companies are increasingly recognizing the value of taking a *portfolio* approach that uses a combination of various methods, tools, and techniques to address their process improvement opportunities. The Six Sigma Process Management methodology is really the fundamental building block for establishing a robust system of management that enables you to continually identify the best possible portfolio of opportunities that will help you achieve your objectives. We will address this topic further in Chapter 4, where we consider approaches to managing a *portfolio of projects across an end-to-end core process.*

So for now, if you are getting "hung up" on the name—or you think that your organization might—remove the issue from the table and come up with a "label" that works for your organization.

You probably recognize some of the crucial questions on page one because they are the same as those that we often ask before, during, and after working on a Lean Six Sigma project.

For simple comparison purposes, let's take a moment to think about the above list within the context of the DMAIC Six Sigma approach. For

---

- BP named their Lean Six Sigma effort "Process Fitness."
- Dell named their Six Sigma effort "BPI" (Business Process Improvement).
- Sun Microsystems named their Six Sigma effort "Sun Sigma."

example, within the *Define and Measure* phases we use methods, tools, and techniques to help us understand what's important to our customers and how we are currently performing in respect of those Critical Customer Requirements (CCRs). In the *Measure* phase, we establish a robust set of performance metrics that we subsequently monitor and report in the *Control* phase. We do this to measure the impact of the solution we have identified and implemented in the *Improve* phase, to ensure that it truly delivers sustainable improvement and value.

So, our *critical questions* are not new. Lean Six Sigma professionals are working in increasing numbers to find answers to these questions for their projects—day in, day out.

However, what we have observed and believe to be relatively new is the way in which these *critical questions* are now starting to be addressed within the context of a company's *core processes*. This is a very different level of application than at a DMAIC project level, which is typically very narrow in scope.

By asking these critical questions at a "core process" level, companies are now increasingly recognizing that their Lean Six Sigma efforts need to address the priority defects within the end-to-end processes that their customers experience every day.

A QUICK OVERVIEW OF DMAIC

Define: What's the problem we're trying to solve? DMAIC is the acronym for the generic Six Sigma problem-solving approach.

Measure: How do we know this is the problem?

Analyze: What's the data telling us about the problem?

Improve: What are the options for addressing the root causes of the problem?

Control: How do we know the solution we've implemented is solving the problem over time?

Many of the organizations that could today be defined as the more mature in their application of Lean Six Sigma approaches have adapted the generic DMAIC construct for their specific purposes.

A relatively common approach is to add an extra step to maximize project benefits. For example:

- Dell uses DMAICR, where "R" stands for "Report Out."
- American Express use DMAICL, where "L" stands for Leverage.

WHAT'S AN "END-TO-END CORE PROCESS?"

"End-to-End Core Processes" are those high-level processes that are the primary drivers of value, satisfaction, and profit.

Understanding your company's "End-to-End Core Processes" is a starting point for developing a process-based model for your entire organization that will enable you, for example, to identify important internal and external functional connections and interfaces.

Note: we will discuss "End-to-End Core Processes" more fully in the next chapter when we offer ideas and suggestions on how to define these processes for your company.

This is a significantly more strategic approach to identifying Lean Six Sigma initiatives and deploying Lean Six Sigma resources than thus far has generally been the case.

We firmly believe that when companies take a systemic program approach to addressing these questions for the "end-to-end core processes" that their customers experience each day, these companies will be able to significantly enhance the value creation of their Lean Six Sigma efforts. We call this systemic program approach *Six Sigma Process Management*.

SIX SIGMA PROCESS MANAGEMENT IS CRUCIAL FOR BUSINESS SUCCESS

Managing processes for optimal performance has always been important. Today's global business environment is characterized by increasingly extended supply chains across multiple organizational functions, third-party partners, and suppliers, in many cases operating across different cultures, time zones, and geographies. Thus it is even more challenging and important for leaders to optimally manage their organization's processes.

To illustrate this point, let's take a very simple example that has nowhere near the operational complexity we have just described. Perhaps you can relate to poor Mr. Smith's experience?

Mr. Smith has to go on a business trip that requires him to stay overnight at a hotel. On arrival, he checks in at the front desk. The receptionist decides to take a phone call from another customer as the receptionist is in the middle of checking him in. Because it's rather late, Mr. Smith decides to go straight to his room and order room service. Lukewarm food is finally delivered 45 minutes later. Anyhow, Mr. Smith decides that he should get some rest right away, as he has a very important meeting the next morning. The following morning, he showers and then goes down to reception to check out, where he finds six other people waiting to check out as well. He's kept waiting for more than 10 minutes.

As he leaves the hotel, Mr Smith complains about his experience to the Duty Manager, who immediately asks one of his team members to take a look at the issues raised. A week or so later, after some initial analysis, the Duty Manager determines the following about the hotel's service delivery:

- 98 percent of Check Ins are defect free.
- 90 percent of Room Service Orders are defect free.
- 99 percent of Hotel Rooms are defect free.
- 92 percent of Check Outs are defect free.

QUICK DEFINITION

Defect: A *defect* is any output that fails to meet a customer requirement.

While the hotel had always considered their service to be quite good, they were really alarmed when they calculated the probability of customers experiencing a totally defect-free hotel stay. By multiplying each of the yield figures for each subprocess together,[3] they realized that in fact, there's only a 80-percent chance of any customer receiving a totally defect-free experience. (See Figure 1-1.)

Perhaps at this point you're starting to wonder what the probability is of your customers encountering a defect in your processes. We suspect they're significantly more complex than this simple example.

OUR BIG HYPOTHESIS (EDUCATED GUESS!)

Our big hypothesis is that in general, for many of the reasons listed above, business processes are severely suboptimized in most organizations today. This is further compounded by our view that "core processes" are rarely perceived as, or managed as, *strategic assets*.

What do we mean by that rather sweeping statement? Our observation is that in most companies, a weak link at best exists between the overall

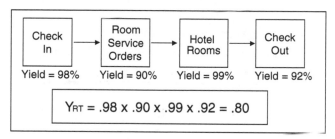

FIGURE 1-1.

business strategy and the *operational strategies, processes, and activities* that are taken day in, day out—supposedly in support of successfully achieving the business strategy.

Today, it's almost certain that if a seamless translation of business strategy to operational execution is being made at all, it is being made within the context of the functional organization. For example, "here's what our business strategy means that Sales now needs to do, or here's what our business strategy means we now need to do in Operations."

In our experience, there is very little evidence to indicate that business strategy is translated into "So, this is what we now need to do across our *end-to-end core processes to successfully achieve our strategic objectives.*" In our experience, most companies—even if they have defined their end-to-end core processes—are not measuring, managing, improving, or redesigning their service delivery using an end-to-end process management approach.

Our view is that strategy execution today is generally taking place within each separate organizational function (e.g., Sales, Operations) as opposed to across *the end-to-end processes* that customers actually experience each and every day throughout the tenure of their relationship with a company. We suspect that this might well be the case with *your* company.

Consequently, we believe that many companies are failing to maximize the value creation opportunities that exist across their end-to-end core processes. This is particularly the case with service and transaction companies where typically, the very nature of the environment and workflow means that *process consciousness* is more challenging to establish and maintain than in a manufacturing environment.

To summarize, we believe that most organizations today are not managing their delivery processes as strategic value-creating assets that foster and achieve increased customer loyalty, but rather as a set of disparate, isolated functional delivery mechanisms that, over time, naturally denigrate customer loyalty. We'll offer the rationale for this in more detail in Chapter 3, where we discuss Kano's ideas about customers' approaches to *satisfaction* over time.

Given that we hold these views, it probably comes as no surprise that we believe a significantly increased emphasis on end-to-end process man-

---

WHY IS IT SO CHALLENGING TO ESTABLISH AND MAINTAIN "PROCESS CONSCIOUSNESS" IN SERVICE AND TRANSACTION ORGANIZATIONS?

- *The end product is less tangible*—It's often information, money, or an experience.

- *The end-to-end process is not visible*—"Work appears on my computer screen. I do my thing, then hit the enter key— I have no idea where it goes next!"

- *Waste and defects are less visible*—How do you sweep up waste in a telephone call center? Within a manufacturing environment, it's often swept up at the end of each shift, in front of everyone!

- *Performance data is not so readily available*—Service processes are commonly not well measured, and available data is often tied up in IT systems, from where it's generally challenging to distil meaningful operational information!

---

agement is required to achieve sustainable business success in this increasingly complex and competitive environment.

TESTING OUR HYPOTHESIS— A SIMPLE ILLUSTRATION

If all of this is getting a bit too theoretical for you, let's take a few minutes to work through a simple practical example. Let's think about the customer acquisition process. This can be considered a *generic core process* in most organizations because most businesses are engaged in acquiring customers!

Figure 1-2 is a simple schematic that shows some high-level generic process activities for acquiring new customers, together with a representation of the various internal functional areas and external suppliers that are involved in this example end-to-end process. In our simple illustration, process participant (A) could represent a company's Direct Marketing Group, or process participant (F) could represent an external third party that phones your newly acquired customers to welcome them to your company.

As you take a look at this relatively straightforward process, think about the end-to-end customer acquisition process within *your* own company and sketch it out, naming the various internal functions and external suppliers as you do so.

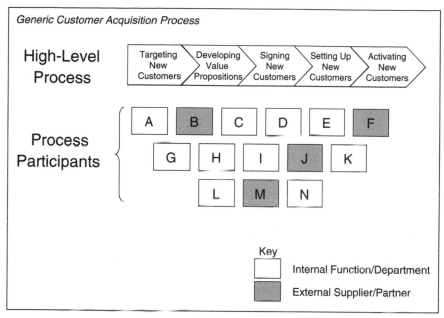

FIGURE 1-2.

Now that you've completed your quick sketch, take a few minutes to reflect on your drawing and consider the following key questions about your process:

1. Does a future-state vision exist for this process—i.e., I know what the key process stakeholders (customers, shareholders, employees, suppliers) require of this process in 3-5 years?
   Yes ☐   No ☐   Don't know ☐

2. Is there a single senior executive process owner who is accountable for performance across the entire end-to-end process?
   Yes ☐   No ☐   Don't know ☐

3. Do the various functional organizations (internal and external) performing roles within this end-to-end process get together regularly to review process performance and prioritize improvement efforts?
   Yes ☐   No ☐   Don't know ☐

4. Is there a robust set of *performance metrics* in place to understand what the end customer actually experiences (e.g., cycle time, defect rate)?
   Yes ☐   No ☐   Don't know ☐

5. Are the *value-adding*,[4] *value-enabling*, and *non-value-adding* activities within this end-to-end process understood?

    Yes ☐   No ☐   Don't know ☐

6. Are business process improvement actions coordinated across this overall end-to-end process, or does each functional organization work on what *they* think is important?

    Yes ☐   No ☐   Don't know ☐

7. Are the people working in this process rewarded for achieving the overall end-to-end process goals (if they exist), or are they rewarded for meeting the specific goals of their own function, with little understanding or focus on the overall performance of the process?

    Yes ☐   No ☐   Don't know ☐

8. Are the outputs from this process seamlessly connected as inputs to other core processes (e.g., ongoing transaction processing, cross-selling) to enable the creation of sustainable value throughout the customer's life-cycle relationship with your company?

    Yes ☐   No ☐   Don't know ☐

If you are able to answer "Yes" to each of the above questions, your company's level of process maturity is relatively high. Alternatively, if you've answered "No" to a number of the above questions, it's likely that you are just getting started on your road to achieving *process maturity!* It's questionable whether any Lean Six Sigma resources you currently have in your company are working on the projects that will really create the *maximum value* for your customers and other key constituencies.

Obviously this simple illustration is not intended as a detailed diagnostic analysis of your company's process maturity. For a start, it only focuses on one core process, but it does serve as a rough guide to help you understand where you currently are.

You might choose to repeat the exercise for other core processes within your company. Incidentally, these are just the very basic questions that can be asked of any process. There are many more questions that can be asked to assess the maturity of your end-to-end process management approach *and* to determine the extent to which processes are managed as strategic assets within your company. We'll come on to these in more detail in the following chapters.

To return to the big picture, given the results of our simple illustration, is it any wonder that organizations find it so challenging to successfully execute business strategy and optimize the value of their Lean Six Sigma efforts in today's environment?

If we seriously think we can continue to measure, manage, and improve processes in the same way that we always have, we should probably be tested for banned substances!

So are there any companies out there that are using this "core-process" focus to drive their Lean Six Sigma business process improvement efforts? The answer is "Yes!"

Here are three such stories—one from a multinational company that chose to refocus its already excellent Six Sigma efforts—another from a multinational company that proactively evolved to a stronger core process focus as part of its implementation "game-plan"—and finally, a smaller UK-based company that decided to take a strong end-to-end core process focused approach from the very start of their Six Sigma implementation effort.

REFOCUSING SIX SIGMA AT GE

GE, a company that in many respects is considered to be one of the most successful implementers of Six Sigma, began to recognize the shortfalls of their functionally (i.e., non-core-process) focused approach several years ago. GE's Six Sigma rejuvenation came about by asking some very fundamental questions of their business:

- What are the key processes we are trying to improve and that will fundamentally change our competitive position (the game changers)?
- What is our entitlement (value of getting to Six Sigma) with those processes, and what is the potential benefit to our business?
- What percent of our Six Sigma resources are devoted to reaching that entitlement?

Based on their answers to these "fundamental questions," they refocused their Six Sigma efforts on:

- The "Game Changers"—The key processes that create competitive advantage:
  - New Product Introduction (NPI)
  - Inquiry to Order (ITO)
  - Order to Remittance (OTR)
  - At the Customer for the Customer (ACFC)
- Achieving quantifiable improvements in these key processes

Interestingly, GE is by no means alone in seeing a need to refocus their Six Sigma efforts in order to maximize the value creation they seek for their Customers and other key Stakeholders.

Shell Gas (LPG) applied *Sigma* (they dropped the *"Six"*!) to its business. Their challenge was to answer a simple question—how best to improve a Liquid Petroleum Gas (LPG) business operating in 50 countries and serving 40 million customers? They initially committed to their Sigma effort for five key reasons:

*   Their continuing drive to improve business efficiency and consistency of delivery on the customer promise;
*   Their belief in the power of process management;
*   The external credibility of (Six) Sigma;
*   The importance of achieving lasting, measurable benefits;
*   The ability to achieve long-term competence development.

They achieved improved bottom-line performance and started to improve their business competencies. However, they realized the need to *evolve* their Sigma effort to the next level in order to significantly strengthen their process focus. This was particularly important because a companywide business thrust on Business Process Standardization was gaining momentum, and within the LPG business, a vision of end-to-end process management already existed. There was also widespread recognition within Shell at this time that they needed to systematically improve their "core-processes" across the business. They also wanted to build upon their initial Sigma foundation. And so the major challenge they faced was how to link these things together into a coherent, results-oriented strategy.

Their answer was to develop an enhanced business Blueprint in which the core processes to deliver value (e.g., Offer to Contract) were identified and used as the basis for the development of an integrated road map. This provided a framework for identifying the next set of projects that were subsequently executed through a variety of Sigma approaches.

All good stuff! However, you don't need to be into a multiyear Lean Six Sigma implementation before the benefits of taking a strong core-process-focused approach can yield results. On the contrary, it's possible to take a Six Sigma Process Management approach from the very start of your Lean Six Sigma implementation. This is exactly what a medium-sized UK-based Financial Services company did when they started their Six Sigma implementation. The leadership team recognized that if their initial "proof of concept" project was to be a successful "launch pad" for Six Sigma, it had to satisfy five key criteria:

*   It had to deliver a significant business impact;
*   It needed to align with, and be supportive of, the company's key operational strategies—one of which was to launch a new credit card;

- It needed to focus on an end-to-end process that was easily defined and understood;
- It needed to have cross-functional impact;
- It had to have very strong senior leadership sponsorship and support.

With these criteria in mind and after initial analysis and the presentation of recommendations, the team was given the mandate to proceed with a Six Sigma effort focusing on the end-to-end New Customer Acquisition process. The project was immensely successful—generating total cost reduction and additional revenue generation benefits of over £1.5 million—not bad for a first "proof of concept" project!

Based upon this success, the relatively small team of six full-time people have now broadened their end-to-end process analysis and infrastructure efforts.

They have defined and agreed upon eight core processes with the senior leadership team and developed performance dashboards for at least half of these, which have enabled them to identify further high-impact and high-priority projects that are now underway. Furthermore, process dashboards are now starting to drive additional demand for Six Sigma capabilities within the organization.

We hope that by taking this little diversion to explain some *real-world* company examples, you are starting to understand the benefits that a Six Sigma Process Management approach can provide to your Lean Six Sigma deployment efforts.

The third question we would like to address in this opening chapter is "How does our proposed approach for achieving business process leadership fit with today's business improvement landscape?" After all, there are so many different approaches out there, you might be forgiven for thinking that this is just one more approach dreamt up by management consultants who are keen to boost their fee revenue!

So how on earth did we end up in this situation of process suboptimization? It's not as if there haven't been approaches over the last 100 years or so to help us improve our business processes! In fact, on the contrary, many approaches, methods, tools, and techniques have been developed.

Before we go any further, perhaps we should take a few minutes to do a quick recap on the history of business process improvement.

So what can we learn from this little history lesson? The first thing that strikes us is that there have been a lot of great approaches, methods, tools, and techniques developed in the last 100 years to help people optimize the way business processes operate. *And* although we've described them in a rather nonacademic way here—you probably noticed that—we are nevertheless deeply respectful and genuinely grateful for the business

MIKE AND ROWLAND'S BRIEF HISTORY OF BUSINESS PROCESS IMPROVEMENT

(with sincerest apologies to Stephen Hawking and Bill Bryson!)

People have been looking to improve things in their lives ever since that poor guy came up with the square-shaped wheel several thousand years ago.

In the interest of time, we'll cut to the chase and focus on approaches that have been developed to improve business process performance during the last 100 years. It goes something like this.

In 1913 there was this smart dude called Henry Ford. You might have heard of him. Anyhow he came up with this pretty neat idea called the Moving Assembly Line. You could think of this as a starting point.

In 1920 Freddie Taylor developed Time and Motion studies to better understand how stuff got done and how long it took. A lot of his ideas are still around in process management today. Then, in 1927 Alfred Sloan and General Motors came up with this approach that they called Flexible Mass Production. That was pretty cool as well.

All of these things led to a need for tools to better control quality, and so in 1931, Walter A Shewhart (Walt to his pals) developed the foundations of Statistical Process Control with his Economic Control of Quality. If you're using Minitab today, you're probably using tools that dear old Walt initially came up with. What a guy!

Anyhow, the U.S. military built upon Walt's ideas and in the 1940s developed further Statistical Sampling techniques. This was followed in the 1950s by Deming and Juran's initial work on Lean manufacturing techniques at Toyota. You've probably heard of these guys!

In the early 1960s, the Japanese Quality Movement was truly born with the work of Taguchi and Ishikawa—the fishbone dude. Then in 1970, Philip Crosby (not the guy with Stills & Nash—remember them?) figured out that Quality is Free! Also, at about the same time Taiichi formalized the Toyota Production System.

During the early 1980s this thing called Total Quality Management came along. It was pretty cool, but while it seemed to make a lot of sense to the quality nerds, the company execs had a hard time figuring out where the value came from.

So in the late 1980s (1987 to be exact) Motorola started to pull together this weird stuff called Six Sigma. (The rest, as they say, is history!) At about the same time ISO and Malcolm Baldridge started their whole assessment thing. This became the foundation for a whole load of other quality assessment frameworks in various countries (Canada, Mexico, across Europe, and the Far East).

In 1989 Bob Camp suggested that we really should be spending more time benchmarking our performance against others—so we all went off benchmarking mad for a while.

And then in 1990, Michael Hammer figured out that companies really needed to be revolutionary as opposed to evolutionary in their approach to reengineering the corporation. He became the darling of the suits (many, although not all, senior execs) for awhile because their gross misinterpretation of his excellent ideas gave them "carte blanche" to slash and burn their way through their own companies, turn in excellent short-term results for their shareholders, and get themselves fat bonuses. Man, what a macho trip that was.

Anyhow, after the slash-and-burn party had finished, people started to wake up with an almighty hangover because they realized that many of them had overlooked one tiny little factor in the reengineering binge they'd just been on, and that was a little unheard of constituency called "customers!"

Meanwhile, GE was making great strides with its Six Sigma efforts. They too eventually realized that customers really needed to have a stronger voice in all this process improvement stuff and so took their efforts to the next level with an initiative called "At the Customer, For the Customer." Now we're getting somewhere!

More recently, people have been tinkering around with integrating Lean, Supply Chain Management methods, complexity reduction techniques, and TRIZ (that Russian fast-path problem solving thing) into Six Sigma to strengthen it further—all pretty cool stuff, but hardly a separate movement in itself!

Anyhow, that just about brings us up-to-date. Welcome to business process improvement in the twenty-first century!

process improvement inheritance that has been handed down to us. Our maximum respect goes to all the people who have contributed and made sacrifices along the way. Thank you!

Second, our view is that there's not a single method or tool out there that in itself will enable organizations to achieve the success they require for their businesses today. As the saying goes, "When you've got a hammer, everything looks like a nail!" So we need to learn how to selectively use the appropriate methods and tools on a situational basis to help us solve problems, address opportunities, and thereby achieve the business results we strive for. We should *never* become slaves to the tools! And as we said earlier, we're not interested in labels (including Six Sigma Process Management)! Who cares what it's called as long as we're able to assemble the best approach to achieve the best results for our customers and key stakeholders?

Third, and in a way, this is the bottom line—getting any of these approaches to work requires exceptionally strong leadership. As the saying goes, "If you want the mouse to go to the left of the cage, don't put the cheese on the right." Hey, who moved my cheese?

So how can we summarize the way in which the ideas you'll read about in this book relate to today's business improvement landscape? Well, we wish we could claim they're completely original, but the truth is they're not! The foundations for many of the core concepts that we're going to be building upon have a strong relationship and lineage with much of what we have just described in our Brief History of Business Process Improvement—key concepts of Customer Focus, End-to-End Process Management, and Managing by Facts and Data.

And, as we discussed at the opening of this chapter, you're probably familiar with many of these approaches through your existing project work. What we're interested in exploring is how these excellent "project" level approaches can be integrated into a companywide "program" level approach that will enable *you* to answer the key questions we've asked so far, for *your* company's core processes—in much the same way as GE asked their fundamental questions for their company.

These "core processes" are after all—good, bad, or indifferent—what your customers experience every single day. These experiences (sometimes referred to as "moments of truth") shape your customers' perceptions and loyalty to your company, their buying decisions, their extent of advocacy for your brand, and ultimately your company's profitability and success.

We had better "Get them right—the first time, every time!"

Achieving business process leadership is immensely challenging, enormously rewarding, and above all, crucial to the future success of your company. If you don't do it, it's just possible that your competitors will! In fact, they may be already.

NOTES

1. Effectiveness can be thought of as the extent to which the "*output*" meets the needs of the customer.

2. Efficiency can be thought of as the quantity of resources required to produce the "*output.*" These typically include such things as people, time, money, and materials.

3. This calculation is known as Rolled Throughput Yield (Y_{RT}). By multiplying the Yield numbers together we reach 0.80 (i.e., 80 percent). This means that there's a 20-percent probability that a customer will experience at least one defect!

4. Process steps and activities can be analyzed and classified in one of three ways:

    (1) Value-Adding steps are those that are essential to deliver the product or service according to Customer requirements.

Value-Adding steps must satisfy three criteria (a) Transforms the item or service toward completion (b) Customers would be willing to pay for it (c) Done right the first time.

(2) Value-Enabling steps are those that allow overall greater effectiveness or efficiency in the process.

(3) Non-Value-Adding steps are those that do not qualify as either value adding or value enabling.

CHAPTER 2

LEADING SIX SIGMA PROCESS MANAGEMENT

We believe that *exceptional* change management skills are required by leaders and those working in *"business process improvement,"* and throughout this book, we use that term in its broadest possible definition. These competencies are necessary to fully realize the *business process leadership* opportunities that exist in most organizations today.

In our view, the number of companies that can legitimately claim to have achieved *"true"* business process leadership can be counted on the fingers of one hand *and*, they're continually improving the performance of their processes as well!

WHAT DIFFERENTIATES COMPANIES THAT ARE PURSUING BUSINESS PROCESS LEADERSHIP?

While the various methods, tools, and techniques available to achieve business process change might be somewhat different from one another, there is one common, unifying theme that's a crucial success factor for all of them, and that's *leadership*!

Achieving *business process leadership* is not just about using the most powerful process management improvement and design/redesign methods, tools, and techniques such as those Lean Six Sigma tools contained within the Process Management toolbox. We'll cover those in the next chapter.

Although these approaches have a key role to play, *like all tools, they are a means to an end and not an end in themselves*. In some companies, this simple fact tends to get overlooked, and process improvement people get caught up in the "beauty" of the tool, or the "application" of the tool, rather than the "end-game" of what they're trying to achieve—namely improved processes that will create significantly enhanced value for their customers and key stakeholders. Perhaps you've witnessed this in your own company?

The companies that are the leading Lean Six Sigma proponents today go way beyond methods, tools, and techniques. At the heart of their approach to *business process leadership* is an acknowledgment that the fundamentals of how their business processes are defined, measured, managed, and continually improved must be radically changed.

The leaders of these companies recognize and understand the value of managing their work flows on an end-to-end basis—from promise to fulfillment. These companies are cutting through functional layers, decision making, operational systems, and old ways of doing things to expose the essential processes and key attributes of those processes that their customers value.

And, once they truly understand how the key things that they make and/or do actually create and deliver value for their customers, they set in place Six Sigma Process Management techniques to help them continually meet (or exceed) those customers requirements. This leadership mind-set requires outstanding vision, commitment, and tenacity.

PROCESS INTELLECT ALONE IS NOT ENOUGH

Interestingly, while we've observed that many people working in organizations understand the need for, and recognize the benefits of, improved process management to optimize their Lean Six Sigma project efforts at an *intellectual level*—after all, it's not in the same league as solving prime number theory—an *emotional disconnect* often exists that prevents those individuals, and therefore their organizations, from really getting process management to stick. Consequently, these companies fail to realize the enormous benefits such an approach can offer.

Why is this the case, especially as the concepts are quite easily understood at an intellectual level? Actually, we think it's quite an understandable human response and is consistent with one of the key questions that must be addressed for everyone involved in any change effort—"What's in it for me?" (WIIFM?)

Also, we shouldn't overlook the fact that we need the very people who are successful in the existing, often functionally oriented, organization to profoundly change the way in which the business (and quite likely their performance) will be defined, measured, and managed. Is it any wonder

While there are many formulas and equations used in Lean Six Sigma approaches, we believe that this simple equation is the most important.

$$R = Q \times A$$

It shows us that Results (R) are a function of the Quality of our Solution (Q) multiplied by the Acceptance (A) of that solution. So, for example, if we have the best possible solution in the world (a 10 out of 10), but we have little acceptance of it by the organization (1 out of 10), the results will be very limited indeed:

$$10 = 10 \times 1$$

However, if we focus our efforts more on increasing the organization's acceptance for our solution (5 out of 10), even at the expense of reducing the functionality of our solution (8 out of 10), the overall results we could expect to achieve would be significantly increased:

$$40 = 8 \times 5$$

In our experience, many organizations relentlessly focus on the *Quality of the Solution* and fall short in achieving the required *Acceptance* for their solution. Consequently, their change efforts fail to achieve the *Results* that are required.

that the natural human instinct is to be skeptical of, or to resist, such an approach?

To maximize your Six Sigma Process Management efforts, you will need to develop an intellectually robust approach and gain the acceptance and buy-in for your approach throughout your organization.

We will explore approaches to address this crucial change management equation throughout our book, but for now we should remember that most organizations have evolved in a very functionally oriented way and, in many cases, for very good reasons.

We should also remember that people don't maliciously design processes to be bad. They just end up that way over time. As you have probably experienced in your working life, even the best-designed operational processes tend to naturally denigrate over time as opposed to improve of their own free will.[1]

WHAT'S MY ROLE?

Your role as a leader in enabling your organization to achieve the optimum results from its Six Sigma Process Management efforts cannot be understated. The environment that you create and continually foster through your everyday actions will have a profound impact on how business process leadership is perceived and, consequently, the results that are achieved.

In today's highly complex and competitive business environment, leaders require exceptional change management skills to be successful in many aspects of business. Simply doing one thing at a time is no longer enough to *"win the game."* As James Collins eloquently describes in "Good to Great," those companies that achieve truly great results are those that have the ability to embrace the "Genius of the 'And' and who refuse the Tyranny of the 'Or.'"

As a leader responsible for a Six Sigma Process Management effort, you will need to do likewise. Take the time, commitment, and energy to focus your resources and your organization on both achieving project successes today, while building a robust process management infrastructure to achieve sustainable business improvements and results in the future.

We often refer to this as getting your deployment balance right between *"projects"* and *"program"*—the two "P"s. You'll need another two "P"s to be successful on your Six Sigma Process Management mission—outstanding *"people"* and a highly robust *"process."*

As a key part of the change effort, senior leaders who successfully implement Six Sigma Process Management recognize that it cannot be simply *adopted* "off the shelf" for their organization, but that it needs to be *adapted, tailored, and integrated* with their company's specific priorities, challenges, culture, resources, and operational constraints.

Successfully navigating and leading your organization through these often challenging and in some cases contradictory and ambiguous scenarios will remain a continual challenge throughout the effort. Well, we never said that achieving Six Sigma Process Management would be easy. If it were, we would probably all be doing it already!

So what are the key things that *you* should consider within the context of *your* own organization to maximize the success of *your* Six Sigma Process Management approach?

To help you, we have identified four crucial change leadership components that we recommend you address on your business process leadership journey. You might already have some of these in your organization today. In other cases, you might just be getting started.

We have provided an introductory section on each of the four crucial change leadership components. We will continue to refer to these key leadership themes throughout the remainder of the book:

1.   Mapping your organization's Process Maturity
2.   Shaping and communicating an integrated Vision and Strategy
3.   Successfully executing your strategy:
    a.   Clearly defining Roles and Responsibilities

    b.   Creating shared accountability for Results

    c.   Establishing the Six Sigma Process Management process hierarchy

4.   Assessing progress and identifying future actions

We have one final comment to share with you in closing this section on Leading Six Sigma Process Management. We certainly don't pretend to have all of the answers on how you can successfully lead Six Sigma Process Management at your organization. After all, we don't know anything about your specific organization. You do!

However, one of our key measures of success for this book is to simply encourage you to think differently about business process leadership, ask questions, and open further discussions on what business process leadership means and how it can be achieved in your organization.

We hope that the following material will provide you with some practical and useful ideas to help guide you and your organization on your Six Sigma Process Management journey towards achieving sustainable business process leadership.

1. MAPPING YOUR ORGANIZATION'S PROCESS MATURITY

Developing a "baseline" picture of your start point on a change journey is always a good thing to do. It enables you to understand the distance you've traveled as the effort progresses, and more to the point, understand how much further you need to go and whether any midcourse corrections are required in order to reach your destination.

The same concept applies equally to your Six Sigma Process Management efforts. You will find it very helpful to assess your process maturity at the start of your Six Sigma Process Management effort, and periodically—perhaps every quarter—throughout your journey.

There are many different ways in which you can map your organization's level of process maturity, from a relatively simple approach—such as the eight questions we asked in Chapter 1 to assess your Customer Acquisition process—to highly complex evaluation techniques that consider many different weighted dimensions and subcategories.

Our preference is to "Keep It Simple!" Your process maturity assessments will need to be structured in such a way that they (a) don't consume vast quantities of resources in their preparation and (b) can be easily communicated and understood by the entire organization, not just a small handful of Quality Ph.D.s in the back room!

In Chapter 5 we share our views on what we strongly believe are the operational characteristics of organizations that have reached the highest levels of process maturity. You might find it helpful to take these main *themes and topics* as you start to develop a process maturity model[2] for your organization.

While we don't see it as our place to tell you which components you should include or exclude in the process maturity model for *your* organization, we can share some ideas with you on how you might shape your model. We'll illustrate our thinking with a simple example as we go.

First, it's helpful to come up with a list of the operational characteristics that you feel are the most important. Once these have been organized into their *themes* and *topics*, they can be listed down the left-hand side of the page. We've shown these as (A) in Figure 2-1. For example, let's assume that Process Leadership is one of our *themes* and End-to-End Process Results Orientation is a *topic*.

Next, it's best if you can create a series of *aspirational statements* to describe what each of these *topics* would ideally look like in your *perfect process world*. We've shown these as (B) in Figure 2-1. Please note that you might be a very long way from this level of process maturity today. If you're not, perhaps your perfect process world isn't quite so perfect! In our example of End-to-End Process Results Orientation, we might include an aspirational statement such as Performance Related Pay is integrally linked to achieving the End-to-End Process "Point of Arrival" (POA). We'll describe what we mean by process POA shortly.

Next you will need to assess your current level of process maturity for each of the topics you've defined. This represents today's process world. We've shown this as (C) in Figure 2-1. In our example, we might describe our current situation as "All Performance Related Pay is made based on meeting functional departmental goals."

You can now see the distance between where you currently are and your process destination. In our example, the journey we need to travel on this particular topic is from a functional, departmental-oriented Performance Related Pay mechanism to a Performance Related Pay mechanism based on the extent to which the End-to-End Process (POA) is achieved.

The final step is to develop two or three carefully constructed interim checkpoints—essentially your journey plan against which you will be able to assess your progress going forward. We've shown these as (D), (E), and (F) in Figure 2-1. These checkpoints should describe increasing levels of maturity for each of the characteristics that you've identified in (A), ultimately leading to your view of the highest level of process maturity for your organization as shown in (B). In our Performance Related Pay example (Figure 2-1) D, E, and F *might* look something like this:

D = All functional process participants understand the value of measuring performance on an End-to-End basis

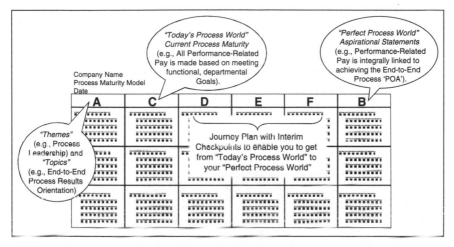

FIGURE 2-1. Schematic of a Process Maturity Model.

E = All functional process participants understand how their Performance Related Pay would change if based on End-to-End performance

F = All process participants have signed up to the End-to-End process goals.

We recommend that you conduct an assessment of your process maturity at regular intervals. We'll describe this further a little later on.

2. SHAPING AND COMMUNICATING AN INTEGRATED VISION AND STRATEGY

We can think about shaping an integrated vision and strategy on two levels (see Figure 2-2).

First, many companies that have embarked upon a significant change effort of any description have found it very helpful to create a *vision* of where they're trying to go. For example, at American Express, the company's vision is "to become the world's most respected service brand." This is a good way to describe what the company is striving for, and it can be a powerful way to mobilize and energize the organization on the journey ahead!

Second, it's crucial that any transformational business improvement effort such as Lean Six Sigma is integrally linked to your organization's overall business strategy—the big things that you're going to do to achieve your vision—and that it is appropriately aligned with any existing business process improvement and/or change initiatives.

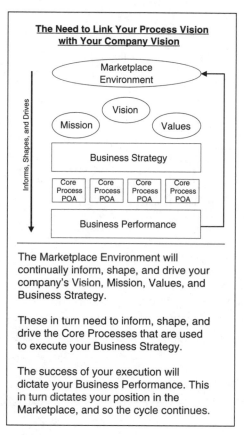

FIGURE 2-2.

The consequences of not establishing such linkages often result in employees asking some very reasonable questions such as "How does this fit with XYZ," or "How serious are we about this," or you might hear statements such as "I don't have time for this; I'm too busy executing our strategy!"

Your employees (and others involved in your end-to-end processes)[3] need to understand that your organization is serious about the effort. This message needs to be communicated and reinforced by the most senior leaders in the organization—continuously and thoughtfully.

Also, as you start to define your "core end-to-end processes"—we'll offer some ideas on how you can do this shortly—it's very important to translate your overall business strategy into a future-state picture for each of your core processes. We'll refer to this as a Process Point of Arrival (POA), as this language seems to be widely used by a number of organizations today.

These Process POAs should explain what each process must look like in order to address the requirements of your business strategy in pursuit of your company's vision. It's really best if your Process POAs can be crafted as a set of five to seven key metrics. In many companies these are referred to as Key Performance Indicators (KPIs). By framing your Process POA in this way, you will be able to track your progress over time and easily communicate successes and areas of focus going forward (see Table 2-1).

As you start to create your Process POAs, you'll probably realize that you don't have all of the data and information that you require. You might be able to use "proxy" measures. These metrics go some way to doing the job

TABLE 2.1 Customer Acquisition End-to-End Process

	Process Performance	
	Today	POA
Applications Processed	10MM	25MM
Sigma Level	3.2	6.0
Process Cycle Efficiency	5%	50%
Unit Cost	10.0c	6.0c
Customer Satisfaction	80%	>95%

One company who has successfully implemented Six Sigma for more than five years has developed an interesting approach to measure the extent to which its leaders demonstrate required Six Sigma supporting behaviours. They solicit feedback from each leader's peer group, subordinates, and superior on the following dimensions:

- Displays public enthusiastic commitment
- Commits sufficient resources
- Creates and maintains a business process management system
- Attends Six Sigma meetings and reviews and positively participates
- Creates a highly talented Six Sigma infrastructure
- Is heavily involved in learning and applying Six Sigma tools/techniques
- Supports Six Sigma training for others
- Helps shape the Six Sigma vision

of the KPIs that you really need, or you might choose, as a placeholder, to simply describe the Process POAs using words until you've obtained the KPI data that you need. In most cases, it's highly likely that one of the first things that you will need to do is to commission some resources to obtain the data that you will require in order to set targets and track performance over time.

Linking your business process leadership journey with your business vision and strategy sends the right message from the start. We're serious about this! Regular and frequent communications and other visible actions from senior leaders will be crucial in reinforcing the company's commitment to the effort.

3. SUCCESSFULLY EXECUTING YOUR STRATEGY

Many factors will directly contribute to, or influence, your ability to successfully execute your strategy. In this section we focus on three key factors that as a leader you will need to take ownership for, and we highly recommend that you do indeed take personal ownership for leading these components. It would send a very poor signal to the organization if you were not actively engaged in these initial important start-up activities:

a.   Clearly define Roles and Responsibilities
b.   Create shared accountability for Results
c.   Establish the Process Hierarchy

(A) CLEARLY DEFINE ROLES AND RESPONSIBILITIES

One of your key responsibilities in establishing Six Sigma Process Management is to ensure that clearly defined roles and responsibilities exist within the organization to drive the effort forward.

While the specific role names might vary from organization to organization, many high-performing, process-managed organizations establish formalized roles similar to the model team structure shown in Figure 2-3. These are likely to be different from the existing roles and responsibilities in your organization, so it is important that you take the time to ensure clarity and understanding.

The *Process Owner* is a senior leader who has ultimate accountability for the End-to-End core process. The Process Owner is generally a member of the company's senior management team, ideally with a reporting line directly to the CEO or COO.

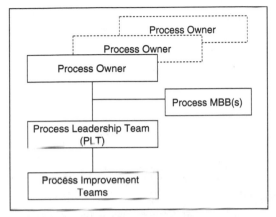

FIGURE 2-3. Six Sigma Process Management "Model" Structure.

The Process Owner's key responsibility is to take personal ownership for leading the effort to achieve the Process POA. As such,

- Establish and lead the Process Leadership Team (PLT);
- Develop the Process POA and journey plan;
- Regularly liaise with other Process Owners to ensure that core process linkages and interfaces are understood and aligned;
- Guide the Six Sigma Process Management implementation;
- Develop and establish Process Governance;
- Make available required resources (e.g., resources for measurement planning and tracking);
- Support Project Teams—remove barriers to cross-functional performance;
- Be a role model—continually display and communicate the crucial cross-functional behaviors required for end-to-end process management.

The *Process Leadership Team* consists of senior functional managers representing all functions (and ideally external companies) involved in the end-to-end core process. The PLT should be actively led by the Process Owner and should collaborate in a collegial manner to guide the Six Sigma Process Management transformation.

The PLT has an evolving role. Initially, their key responsibilities are to:

- Participate in defining the Process POA for the core process;
- Establish the overall process architecture;

- Provide resources for "infrastructure" efforts—e.g., Voice of Customer feedback, Measurement systems, Process documentation;
- Identify and/or approve Lean Six Sigma projects;
- Actively sponsor improvement projects and ensure transfer to "Control."

As the Six Sigma Process Management effort matures, this team's role evolves to support and sustain *Process Governance*, at which point their key responsibilities are to:

- Review process performance using the Health of the Process dashboard. (We'll describe this in later chapters.)
- Monitor and guide the development of new scorecards and metrics;
- Assess progress on closing data gaps;
- Manage the project portfolio:
  - Identify, prioritize, and charter new improvement opportunities;
  - Assess progress on improvement plans;
  - Conduct project tollgate reviews;
  - Implement corrective actions;
- Work with Enablement Processes to optimize results such as financial controls, IT support. (We describe these more fully on p. 33.)
- Manage the Change Communication and Engagement activities such as communicating the process POA, regular updates on process performance, and details of project successes.

The Master Black Belt(s) (MBBs) should ideally be assigned to work with the Process Owner and the Process Leadership Team. As a key contributing

---

ADAPTING AN EXISTING MANAGEMENT STRUCTURE

Many organizations have well-established groups such as "Quality Councils." Some still remain from the days of Total Quality Management.

While these "Councils" are responsible for much of the same actions as the PLT, they tend to be functional and might cover multiple processes.

As your organization transitions to become a process-based organization, the governance structure will need to change. You will want to avoid multiple layers of management that provide direction and the resulting exponential growth in meetings and PowerPoint presentations!

You will need to establish the right balance of functional and process reporting. Regardless of the title, the activities and tasks listed here will need to be carefully and thoughtfully managed.

member and participant of the Process Leadership Team, their key responsibilities are to:

- Operationalize the Process POA by developing detailed plans, often known as multigenerational plans;
- Develop and execute end-to-end process measurement plans to ensure that robust dashboard data is available for decision making;
- Support benchmarking initiatives;
- Manage the end-to-end process project portfolio on a day-to-day basis—prepare updates for process review meetings;
- Align and sequence Lean Six Sigma projects for maximum impact;
- Provide expertise in advanced improvement methods, tools, and techniques;
- Conduct quarterly assessments of progress towards *process maturity*;
- Provide day-to-day guidance to Improvement Teams.

Improvement Teams are commissioned by the Business Process Leadership Team to address process improvement opportunities. Their key responsibilities are to:

- Further develop and refine Lean Six Sigma Project Charters and validate the project rationale/value;
- Select the appropriate improvement approach and level of investigation to develop effective solutions;
- Maintain communication with the Process Leadership Team;
- Drive projects to successful completion;
- Provide documentation of team efforts such as progress reports and project storyboards.

(B) CREATING SHARED ACCOUNTABILITY FOR RESULTS

To ensure that the organization has the right execution and performance focus, many companies establish clearly defined objectives and accountabilities for achieving results in a way that is relevant at a business unit and/or functional/departmental level, and at an individual level. The reason for this approach is that the company Vision, Business Strategy, and Process POAs are at a very high level. While these are crucial for mobilizing the organization, they really aren't specific or detailed enough to be executed at a detailed task level within the process, and so they need to be translated into goals and accountabilities that are both meaningful and manageable. SMART[4] goals are a very good way to drive your strategy execution!

In fact, the process of converting our Process POAs into specific and detailed goals for process participants is best accomplished through two key steps. First, we need to translate the Process POA into a set of strategic process objectives framed within a multigenerational plan. Second, once this has been completed, we can then establish tasks and accountabilities at a sufficiently detailed level to be executable by process participants at all levels of the organization.

There are various ways in which objectives and accountabilities can be established, and approaches vary from company to company. As with Vision and Strategy, the most effective approaches are those that leverage existing established and formalized organizational performance management systems such as your goal-setting and performance appraisal processes.

Many change efforts falter at this point because companies do a poor job of seamlessly linking their Vision with the jobs that people are asked to perform.

The bottom line is that senior leaders need to be continually and visibly engaged in driving and sponsoring their organization's Six Sigma Process Management efforts. It tends not to work so well when leaders just sit behind their desks and "demand that their results be brought to them on the first of each month!"

(C) ESTABLISHING THE PROCESS HIERARCHY

Depending on your company's existing level of *process maturity*, it's highly likely that one of the very first things the Process Owner and the newly established Process Leadership Team will need to do at the start of their Six Sigma Process Management journey will be to establish a common understanding of their company's core processes.

The output from this effort is often referred to as an Enterprise Level Map, or Enterprise Activity Model—and no, it has nothing to do with a floor plan or scale model of the Starship Enterprise! In this introductory section, we'll explain what it is and the role that leaders need to take in creating it. In the next chapter we'll explain how to do it!

Creating an Enterprise Level Model is a crucial initial step on your journey to establishing Six Sigma Process Management. It will provide you with the fundamental framework that you will need to optimize your processes using the various methods, tools, and techniques available going forward.

Think of the rationale for it in this way: If you don't understand what your company's core end-to-end-value creating processes are, how can you determine the extent to which value is being truly created?

Although it seems rather obvious, we often find that many companies do not have a commonly held understanding of their core processes. We often find that if such process understanding and documentation exists at all, it's generally in the hands of one group (more often than not, the IT department!) and generally, is not well communicated, understood, and accepted. Therefore, and most importantly, it's not used throughout the organization to measure, manage, and improve the customer experience!

At this point we should describe exactly what we mean by "process documentation" because there's a real danger that business leaders hear this term and start to see cash disappearing fast from their organization, only to be replaced by some nicely drawn flowcharts!

Developing enterprise-level process documentation is not about mapping every single process to the nth degree. It's about establishing a process construct —starting at the Enterprise level—as a basis for understanding those processes that create the most value for your Customers and key Stakeholders (see Figure 2-4).

Note the distinction made between Core Processes —those that directly create value and product movements—and Enablement Processes, those that *enable* Core Processes to create value. This distinction is an important one and is necessary to understand within your own organization.

The objectives of this company's Enterprise Activity Model were to:

• Establish a common "process" language;

• Create a common understanding of "process;"

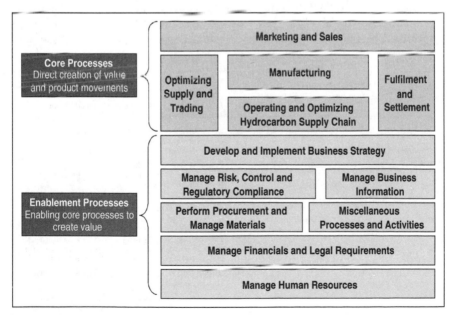

FIGURE 2-4. An Enterprise Activity Model from a multinational integrated oil company.

- Promote the process-oriented organization and culture;
- Promote commonality and standardization of their process;

To better understand their processes, they also developed a series of definitions to further decompose and analyse their processes (see Figure 2-5).

This process definition is a crucial starting point for better understanding how value is created for your Customers and other key Stakeholders—and for prioritizing your future Six Sigma Process Management efforts.

ASSESSING PROGRESS AND IDENTIFYING FUTURE ACTIONS

As with any journey, you will periodically want to look at your route map to understand where you have been, where you currently are—and perhaps most importantly—where you need to go next.

There are several approaches that can enable you to do this. In Chapter 4, we focus on how you can assess progress and identify future actions as part of the *governance* of your end-to-end core processes. In this chapter we will describe how you can regularly assess progress of your organization's overall process maturity.

It's really quite simple. We recommend that each quarter an assessment is conducted to determine progress and identify immediate areas of focus. This is generally best done with a degree of independence—perhaps conducted by two or three MBBs assigned to another core process—and

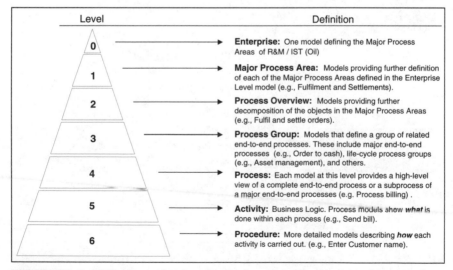

Level	Definition
0	**Enterprise:** One model defining the Major Process Areas of R&M / IST (Oil)
1	**Major Process Area:** Models providing further definition of each of the Major Process Areas defined in the Enterprise Level model (e.g., Fulfilment and Settlements).
2	**Process Overview:** Models providing further decomposition of the objects in the Major Process Areas (e.g., Fulfil and settle orders).
3	**Process Group:** Models that define a group of related end-to-end processes. These include major end-to-end processes (e.g., Order to cash), life-cycle process groups (e.g., Asset management), and others.
4	**Process:** Each model at this level provides a high-level view of a complete end-to-end process or a subprocess of a major end-to-end processes (e.g. Process billing) .
5	**Activity:** Business Logic. Process models show *what* is done within each process (e.g., Send bill).
6	**Procedure:** More detailed models describing *how* each activity is carried out. (e.g., Enter Customer name).

FIGURE 2-5. Definitions of various levels of process decomposition from a multinational integrated oil company.

in a spirit of collaboration. This is not an audit on behalf of those nice people from the tax authorities!

The approach that works best in our experience is for the assessment team to review relevant data and then conduct short (30-45 minute) interviews with key players representing all levels of the organization.

The framework used for the assessment should be the Process Maturity Model, and the key output from the assessment is an understanding of where the organization currently is *vis-a-vis* the aspirational statements described in (B) of your model, together with recommendations on specific areas of focus for the coming 90 days (see Figure 2-6).

Such an approach helps you see progress from assessment to assessment and helps you ensure that momentum is established and maintained throughout your journey.

SUMMARY

Truly outstanding leadership, courage, and commitment will be required to realize the changes that are necessary for your business to achieve the process leadership necessary to compete successfully in the future.

This is not a journey for the fainthearted. Neither is it a journey for those leaders who can only see, want to see, or are rewarded only to see and manage 12 months ahead. Yes, apparently there are some still out there!

This is a journey to what we believe is for many, a brave, new, unexplored world. It will require leadership, passion, conviction, and above all,

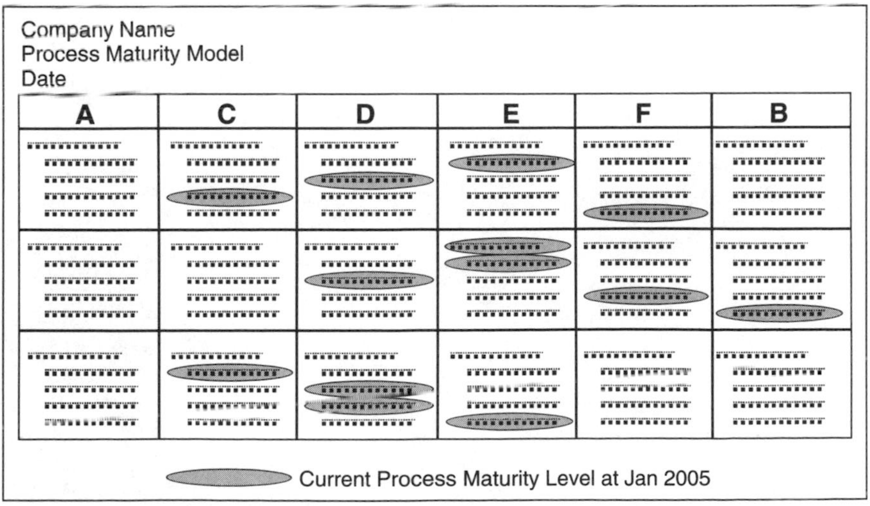

FIGURE 2-6. Schematic of Process Maturity Model updated with maturity assesments findings at January 2005.

a willingness to challenge the "status quo" and take a leap of faith into the unknown. We recognize that this will not be a journey for everyone.

NOTES

1. Customers' expectations tend to increase over time, quite often the *"gap"* between process performance and the ability to meet customers' expectations gets bigger over time. We'll explore Kano's ideas on this further in the next chapter.
2. Remember—all models are wrong, but some are useful!
3. Such as third-party suppliers, vendors, and partners.
4. SMART = Specific, Measurable, Attainable, Relevant, and Timebound!

CHAPTER 3

WHAT IS THE SIX SIGMA PROCESS MANAGEMENT METHODOLOGY?

In this chapter, which forms the heart of our book, we detail a step-by-step methodology for implementing a process management system within the context of the standard Six Sigma DMAIC model. The definition of DMAIC was presented as an insert earlier in Chapter 1 and stands for Define, Measure, Analyze, Improve, and Control. In this chapter, we also outline how many of the same tools used in a Lean Six Sigma project can also be used to help you establish the process management system.

While the Six Sigma DMAIC framework is not new, it is most commonly associated with Lean Six Sigma project execution. In many companies the application of Lean Six Sigma has been limited as a methodology only for improvements within existing processes on known problems. Soon organizations have completed projects for the more glaring defects often without seeing any appreciable impact in customer satisfaction. In the more mature deployments of Lean Six Sigma, the organization's leadership has been able to apply the concepts of Voice of the Customer, process understanding, and rigorous analytics in more creative ways. These companies begin using the Lean Six Sigma concepts in conjunction with their core processes as a framework for deploying process management.

Other companies we have worked with have chosen to create a new acronym in place of, or to adapt, DMAIC for their internal methodology to differentiate a process management project from a process improvement project. Those quality types have been creating cute acronyms for almost 70 years! It is not as important to focus on the acronym as the goal of the effort.

As we have previously stated, the key point is that most advanced or mature deployments have discovered the need for a process management methodology to optimize their improvement, design, and/or redesign methods.

PROCESS MANAGEMENT AT CISCO SYSTEMS

Cisco Systems recently embarked on a global change initiative to significantly strengthen its process focus. Their selected Process Management method is adapted from DMAIC. They use Define, Measure, Analyze, and Control tools and techniques to help identify project opportunities within their core processes.

In each of the DMAIC phases of this section we have included a comprehensive checklist to help guide your Six Sigma Process Management effort. Creating these lists presented us with a challenge in providing you with a robust road map while trying very hard not to be prescriptive and inflexible. You will find that many steps can be done concurrently versus sequentially, and others might already be in place from your previous improvement activities. We will try to point out the opportunities and choices you have as you follow this road map. For example, let's say that you have organized an enterprise process model as described in Chapter 2 from a previous Y2K technologies effort or even from your more recent Sarbanes-Oxley initiative. This would allow you to skip the part of the Define phase, which covers Understanding your Process. However, if you are unsure as to how viable the previous efforts have been at documenting your processes, then review that section for detail information on how to create your enterprise architecture and document it appropriately. Here is a simple tip. Read the key questions we have provided at the start of each of the following sections below. If you can adequately answer that question, then read that section as background information only.

There are two more instructions we need to give you. First is that many of these tasks can be done simultaneously, although they have been written here in a sequential format. We have tried to identify areas of flexibility and have identified activities that can be done concurrently where possible throughout this chapter. If, however, a task must be preceded by another we have mentioned that as well. The second instruction is that some tasks are iterative. For example, we recommend that you create a document we will show you called a Six Sigma Process Management Charter for each initiative. At first pass you will not have a lot of the information to complete this document. As you progress through the various steps, you will gain the additional information needed to complete the document. There are a few activities such as these that require a simple revisit along the way.

Finally, we have tried to be consistent in calling a Six Sigma Process Management effort an initiative versus a project. The term project as we use it is for the improvement effort that is spawned from the Six Sigma Process Management effort. However, some companies treat these initiatives as separate projects in themselves. This scenario usually occurs when an organization has already defined its enterprise and level-1 process hierarchy and are engaging teams to drill down in specific process areas while others are simultaneously running Lean Six Sigma projects. This is more often found in companies that are further along in their deployment and have built up a considerable amount of experience.

AN OVERVIEW OF DMAIC FOR PROCESS MANAGEMENT

In Chapter 2 we presented a brief definition of DMAIC as it relates to executing Lean Six Sigma Improvement projects. Here we have chosen to use the Define, Measure, Analyze, Improve, and Control steps to outline how a Six Sigma Process Management system can be established. The DMAIC acronym can be thought of for now as a Six Sigma "industry" standard.

QUICK DEFINITION

Define: Where are we starting and why?

Define: In Define you begin by identifying your key business processes and subprocesses that meet your customer's needs. For example, at a high level you might have a key business process for customer acquisition. During the Define phase, you will identify the crucial subprocesses that combine to make that process successful. Examples of those subprocesses might be Sales Planning or New Product Engineering. Each of these subprocesses will have multiple layers of subprocesses depending on the complexity and size of the company.

What you will most likely find different from many previous efforts are those crucial words, "customer's needs." As with all Business Process Improvement efforts, it begins and ends with the customer! You determine what the customer requires of each process in a very systematic way. These tasks are commonly called finding the "Voice of the Customer" or your "Critical to Customer" requirements. In fact, the Voice of the Customer is in some ways a misleading term because quite often you will find that a process has many different Customers' Voices, each representing the requirements of a specific segment or subsegment. The exercises we will cover might often cause you to rethink your process structure and lead you to a new definition of your crucial processes. This is a positive change that you must encourage. While you begin the customer journey in the Define phase, it continues throughout the entire path. You also have to organize the effort in Define, as you would with any project team.

QUICK DEFINITION
_____

Measure: Understand the process, the customer, and their voices.

Measure: During the Measure phase, you document these processes and determine what, where, and how to measure the performance of that process. These tasks are commonly called finding the "Voice of the Process." This will also lead to a substantial change in your understanding of your business. As we mentioned in Chapter 2, we often hear groans from many companies when we mention process mapping at this point. All too often these efforts have taken many resources and time while providing little in return. The goal here is different in that the effort will be a stepping stone to later efforts that do provide value.

Most businesses have done a good job at defining their productivity measures in their high-volume functional areas. The opportunity here will be to define and validate a new set of customer-focused metrics in their core business processes.

QUICK DEFINITION
_____

Analyze: What are the best improvement opportunities?

Analyze: In the Analyze phase you find the gap in these "voices." A gap is where your process performance fails to meet your customer expectations. This becomes your project opportunity pipeline (POP)! This is also where you begin to develop in process metrics that tell you proactively how you are performing at meeting your customer's needs.

QUICK DEFINITION
_____

Improve/Control: Drive and manage change!

Improve/Control: The Improve phase is where you implement the Process Management System and begin to drive Lean Six Sigma projects to improve the Critical to Customer metrics. The Control phase links to the governance structure discussed in Chapters 2 and 4 and will be responsible for integrating your various Lean Six Sigma activities in order to optimize the value each brings to the table.

THE DEFINE PHASE

Objective Statement: The objective of the Define phase is to establish the team for the end-to-end initiative to scope the relevant processes and begin to understand your customers' requirements.

Structure: There are three main sections in the Define phase: Beginning the Effort, Understanding your Process, and Understanding your Customer and Stakeholder.

BEGINNING THE SIX SIGMA PROCESS MANAGEMENT EFFORT

Key questions to answer:

1. Where do we start?
2. How do I organize and kick off the initiative?
3. Who should be on the team?
4. What training is needed?

DEFINE THE FOCUS

The first step is to define the area of focus. This is the start of your deployment plan. This links directly back to the enterprise architecture outlined in Chapter 2. If the Process Leadership Team has already focused on which process areas to work on, then you can proceed to the next step.

Take, for example, an enterprise-level process such as Order to Cash. This process might have several level-1 processes such as Sales Entry, Customer Data File Creation/Updates, Production Scheduling, all the way through Statement Printing and Receipt of Cash. You will need to decide if you have sufficient resources to cover all of these process areas or if you are going to break the project up into phases based on some relevant prioritization criteria. You might even want to use what is often called a multigenerational plan.

Now you need to engage the team and set time lines for delivering results. The team should have as a minimum a project manager, a Lean Six Sigma resource, and a relevant number of knowledgeable resources from the process areas. In addition it is valuable for the resources to attend some training on Six Sigma Process Management. We often recommend a workshop-based "train then do" program with multiple project-based exercises. The training is more valuable if the project team can begin to work on their Six Sigma Process Management effort in the classroom environment. This is one of the reasons that most Lean Six Sigma training is delivered in a multiweek format over several months.

PROCESS OWNERSHIP

The next crucial task is to define the owner of the process. We have discussed this before in Chapter 2, and it is essential to verify that it has been completed in the Define phase. The Process Owner should be at a high enough level to have visibility of the end-to-end process. They should also be able to influence change within the process and have a stake in the game. This means they will benefit from the results of this effort. Pande, Cavanagh, and Neuman describe the role in their book *The Six Sigma Way* as, "This is the person who takes on a new, cross-functional responsibility to manage an end-to-end set of steps that provide value to an internal or external customer." The Process Owner will then drive the remaining tasks in this step of the Define phase.

The process owner now has to identify the objectives. This is quite different from a Lean Six Sigma improvement project, where you typically focus on a single defect and the Process Owner is involved only as it applies to that project. Here you are looking to establish a process measurement system and a project pipeline, so how should I define my objectives? The objective is to create a scorecard of your most crucial customer-focused measures and a portfolio (a fancy word for list or spreadsheet) of your most crucial project opportunities.

CHARTER THE EFFORT

The initial effort in any Lean Six Sigma project, whether it is an improvement effort, a design effort, or a process management effort, is called "Chartering the Initiative." This effort usually revolves around completing a document called a Project Charter. The purpose of this chartering effort is to communicate the ownership of the effort, set clear objectives for the team, define the area of focus, and establish the team and initial time lines. The Charter also helps to sell the compelling reason for change and answer the big *why*! Why do we need to do this?

The common charter document for a Six Sigma Process Management effort would normally contain the following:

- A brief paragraph establishing the purpose of the initiative
- An explanation as to why this is important
- Data describing how well or poorly we are performing now
- The goals or objectives
- A list of everyone involved, from Process Owner to Subject Matter Expert
- Any financial benefit
- Any implementation costs if known

XYZ Company   **SSPM Charter**

Enterprise Level Process Area: Order to Cash
Process Focus Area: End-to-End Initiative

Overview: The Order to Cash process is a critical Enterprise-level process consisting of 11 different level-1 processes crossing 7 business units and incorporating 15 different critical customer touch points. Customer surveys and complaint data have shown this process to create more dissatisfaction than any other process. Over 100 complaints have been logged in the invoicing process alone. A recent benchmarking study done by the Peter W. Copper consulting firms has shown our costs for processing orders to be 15% higher than our nearest competitor. OTC is also ranked as the number-1 strategic priority by our technologies enablement team for transformation.

Objective: Document the level-1 processes and identify the critical process metrics, failures, and improvement opportunities.

Process Owner: Herb Wells
Core Team members: Carlos Bocock, William "Trip" Jones and Mari Ann Mokrey. SMEs to be determined.

Timeline: To be completed by end of 1st quarter. Status updates to be provided to the PLT every third Tuesday.

FIGURE 3-1.

A sample of a Process Management charter from XYZ Company is shown in Figure 3-1.

COMMUNICATE AND ENGAGE

This task is to communicate the compelling reason for change. The truth about any quality or process improvement activity is that it requires 80-percent change management and 20-percent methodology. Communication has to be constant and from the right levels. While this type of effort is easier when sponsored by high levels of leadership, you will still need to have the business case for those leaders to sell the effort. Verify that your key stakeholders are engaged either within the team or as a member of the PLT.

A tremendous source of information to make your case for change is from capturing data on how well you are doing compared to your competition, where you want to be as a company, and from information on what your customers think about how well you are doing. You can see how to capture this information in the Understanding your Customers section below.

The typical charter document tries to capture these crucial elements in a one-page synopsis. Remember that the charter is a living document that you must refresh with additional facts as you discover them. At this stage you might not have all of these details.

ESTABLISH THE PROJECT MANAGEMENT PROCESS

This is simply the project management of your Six Sigma Process Management initiatives. The Tollgate review process is a similar construct to the one used for project reviews in Lean Six Sigma projects. When you tollgate an initiative, it means you have established a regularly scheduled review to evaluate the completion of key project tasks and deliverables by each phase of the DMAIC process.

UNDERSTANDING YOUR PROCESSES

Key questions to answer:

1. Have my Enterprise and level-1 Processes been identified?
2. Which process should I begin with?
3. How can I begin to better understand the process?
4. Are there existing Process maps available for use?

WHAT IS A PROCESS?

A process is a series of steps that is designed to produce a result. It transforms input to output in a definable, repeatable, and measurable way. In business this is usually defined as a product or service. We use many processes in our day-to-day lives without ever realizing these are processes. We have processes we call upon from memory when we wake up and get ready in the morning, organize our own work throughout the day, and make dinner in the evening. The concepts of basic process management were well researched back in the late 1980s. However, they lacked the additional power of Lean Six Sigma for performance improvement. The two concepts, when brought together, provide the synergy for real accomplishment.

In a large global enterprise it can be a daunting task to identify your processes. This effort is often seen as having no value added to the business. This is again where Lean Six Sigma has changed the way people think. You can directly tie performance improvements measured in dollar savings and increased customer satisfaction.

TABLE 3-1.

PROCESS EXAMPLE	SERVICE OR PRODUCT DEVELOPED
Billing	Invoice
Fabricating	Window frames
Transportation	Delivery of goods or services
Hiring	Providing labor

At the highest level, any process begins with a request for that product or service by a customer and ends with delivery of that product or service to that customer. Here are a few simple examples (see Table 3-1).

HOW DO PROCESSES WORK?

Processes connect through various functional areas, which perform the required tasks in developing the product or service. You must first understand the higher end-to-end process level before you can begin to analyze the lower functional components. A service process might have multiple points of entry such as mail, phone, or email where the customer is engaged. If the process is truly different from end to end, you should identify it as a separate process. However, in many cases it is really just different variations of the same process. Processes are also often mistakenly viewed as a specific function. Very few functional areas in a large business truly house an end-to-end process. More often, like functions from different processes are grouped together to create productivity efficiencies. An example would be your procurement department, where you staff people experienced in the methods of purchasing and not necessarily knowledgeable in the item they are purchasing.

It is also important to note that leadership, technology, and HR are process enablers to your customer-facing processes and can be confused as the process itself. This is extremely important to service and nonprofit processes. An example would be in a call center environment, where the majority of investment dollars are spent on technology, which can become the sole focus of improvement. In that situation, change is often seen as only technology development. By taking a step back and looking at the processes (making a sale, tracking a shipment, assisting a customer, etc.), you see multiple opportunities to improve the process, not just the technology that enables the process. For those who work in technology, the opposite can often happen. They focus solely on problems they see within their internal customer's process and do not see the process problems within their own support processes (project cost allocation, server charge-outs, etc.).

OUTSIDE-IN VERSUS INSIDE-OUT

There are a number of ways in which you can start to shape your company's end-to-end core processes. For example, you could take a life-cycle approach, in which you consider the key things that your company provides to Customers throughout the tenure of their relationship with you. This approach typically identifies core processes such as:

- Develop New Products and Services
- Acquire Customers
- Process Customer Transactions
- Process Remittances
- Handle Customer Inquiries

This is certainly a very good way to start your Six Sigma Process Management effort and will yield results. However, this is fundamentally an Inside-Out approach—you're really shaping your core processes from the perspective of what the organization does to address its Customers' needs. *We don't know about you, but we're not sure that as "Customers" we like the thought of being "Acquired!"*

This leads us to an even more powerful customer-driven approach that you can take to shape your core processes, and it's achieved by taking more of an Outside-In approach.

We can continue to take a life-cycle perspective as before, but we consider the delivery processes from the Customer's experience and perspective. So, for example, rather than use language such as Acquire Customers, we might define the processes more in the way that customers experience their interactions with our organization. For example, as customers we might:

- Apply for the product
- Use the product
- Pay for the product
- Upgrade the product
- Update my contact and financial details
- Get my inquiry or dispute resolved

In shaping your company's processes in this way, you will create a framework that drives a much stronger customer-oriented way of thinking based on *their experiences.*

IDENTIFY YOUR PROCESSES

This leads you to ask the question, "How do you identify processes? And "What are our high-level business processes?" In order to answer this question, it usually requires a bit of facilitated discussion with personnel familiar with the business involved. Although it would seem easy to define what a business unit does, often the people "in" the process have the most difficult time keeping the discussion at a high enough level to see the major flow of steps. That is often the reason for needing an outside facilitator to conduct the initial discussion.

A framework we like to use in order to begin this discussion is to minimize the entire company into a three-to-five-step enterprise-level flowchart. Figure 3-2 shows a simple chart that can be used to start your discussion.

This is an abbreviated version of the Order to Cash process previously discussed. Now obviously this is an extremely oversimplified view of the world, but it allows you the context to conduct the next level of discussion. The first question to ask is, "What is included in each of these boxes?" Begin to list your high-level processes under each box. Stickies can also be used with this exercise. Make sure that you differentiate between what a process is and what a function is. Remember to use the "Jerry Garcia" principle with the team at this point. The Jerry Garcia principle states, "Keep them as high as you can for as long as you can!"

Next ask the question, "What is missing in these three boxes?" Most commonly the responses you will receive will be the enabling processes such as technology, operations management, and resource management.

These high level process discussions will give you a framework for your organization that can then be drilled down to specific subprocesses. The combinations of these enterprise, high-level, and lower-level processes are called your process hierarchy. (See Figure 3-3.)

The challenge when identifying lower-level processes is to avoid thinking functionally. We often find it useful to begin these discussions with a statement like, "Tell me what this unit does for the customer." The next question would be, "What product or service do we provide for our customers and how do we do it?" The team then begins to identify the customer-specific processes that deliver these products or services. The resulting

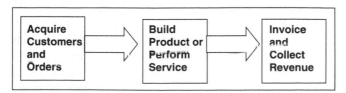

FIGURE 3-2.

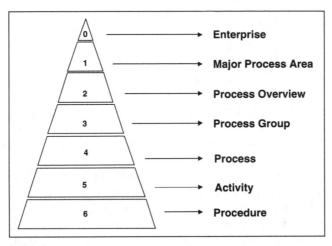

FIGURE 3-3.

grouping should define many of your next-level processes. The team can then begin to discuss the organization's primary functional units, how they interact with each other, and where they fit in the process. Table 3-2 demonstrates the linkage between product/service and your process hierarchy.

PRIORITIZE YOUR EFFORT

Many organizations will be tempted to spend a tremendous amount of time at this point trying to outline their complete organization and to get their process hierarchy perfect. The purpose of this step is primarily to get you organized for your following activities. The process identification exercise is not an end to itself; keep your Six Sigma Process Management teams moving forward using the checklist. After you have completed the enterprise level-one option, what may be more efficient is for you to take one specific process area and detail it down to a lower level to use as an example for the rest of the organization. In this case where a single high-level process has been selected for drill down, you will need to establish a process prioritization matrix to assist in the choice of which process to select. Table 3-3 is an example of a Process Prioritization matrix.

Since you have not gathered your Voice of the Customer information yet, this matrix will evolve. The Voice of the Customer is covered in the next section, Understanding the Customer. Soon we will discuss how to gather and use the customer's feedback to update this matrix.

Remember at this stage to ensure that you have communicated to the organization what you are doing and why this is beneficial to them and their customers. Appropriate visibility and sponsorship must be constant for the teams in order for them to be successful.

TABLE 3-2.

	MANUFACTURING	SERVICE	NOT FOR PROFIT
Organization Type	Industrial plumbing supply manufacturer	Regional banking operation	Local public library
Product	Large industrial application well fittings	Personal and small business checking accounts	Books, periodicals, and mixed media
High-Level Process Example	Customer acquisition	Client account information	Materials acquisition and setup
Low-Level Process Example	1. Market intelligence	1 Statement creation and delivery	1. Order input and tracking
	2. Bid creation and approval	2. Online account access	2. Acceptance and verification
	3. Engineering specifications and quality review	3. Transaction research and dispute management	3. Catalogue setup

TABLE 3-3.

PROCESS NAME	CUSTOMER IMPACT	STRATEGIC IMPACT	EASE OF IMPLEMENTATION	TOTAL
NOTES	HIGH = 5, LOW = 1	HIGH =5, LOW = 1	BEST = 5, LEAST = 1	SUM
A	5	3	1	9
B	4	4	4	12
C	2	4	2	8
D	5	5	3	13

VIEWING THE PROCESS

The first view you want to create is called the high-level SIPOC diagram, which depicts your customer, supplier, and major process phases. This is a useful tool for documenting your high-level process. It stands for Supplier, Input, Process, Output, and Customer

WHAT IS THAT CALLED AGAIN?

In some Companies the term *SIPOC* has been flipped to spell *COPIS* in order to ensure that the customer comes first in the process diagram! The general structure is the same as the one shown in the example in this section. Another creative variation is called *SIRPORC*, where a section for requirements has been added between the Input and the Process and between the Output and the Customer.

All processes, even internal ones, follow this flow in the process value chain. You receive something of value from your supplier. You process it and then forward to your customer. The SIPOC diagram is useful for displaying these handoffs. It is particularly good at communicating this at a high level to leadership. Figure 3-4 is an example of a SIPOC diagram from the University of Central Florida.

There are a few limitations of this tool to consider. If you are trying to create a detailed process diagram that crosses through multiple functions, this chart becomes very awkward. Also if you wish to use the SIPOC as a documentation tool where you include process data, system linkages, and defect information, the SIPOC structure becomes unwieldy. Most commonly companies use the SIPOC as a direction finder. However, when

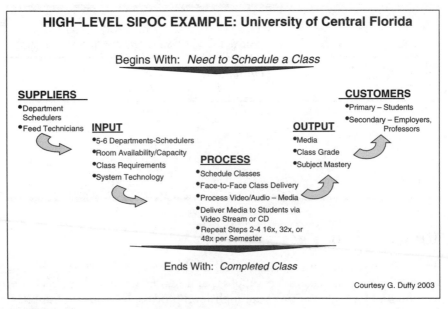

FIGURE 3-4.

XYZ COMPANY

Process Boundaries for the Order to Cash Process:

START	END
Receipt	Deposit
of Order	Cleared

---

combined with the detailed process flow diagram described later in the measure phase, it becomes a powerful combination.

PROCESS BOUNDARIES

Where does your process start and where does it end? This is what we mean by process boundaries. For example, you are involved in establishing a process management system for the product return process in a large manufacturing company. What initiates the process? Is it the receipt of order from the customer or some other action? Validate that this is where you want to begin. Are you going to look at the process only through the merchandise returns subprocess, or are you going to include the supporting accounting processes or even the product replacement process? These are decisions you have to make as you establish your process management system. You can also use the prioritization tools we discuss in this book. This helps you define who needs to be involved and where the action is! This also shows you where the handoffs occur and can lead you to potential failures.

This effort might appear strongly related to several of the steps above, as it should be. As we discussed before, even though we are presenting these steps in a sequential order, many of these Define phase steps can be done concurrently.

UNDERSTANDING YOUR CUSTOMER

Key questions to answer:

1. Do I know what my customers expect?
2. How do I uncover my customer's expectations?
3. How do I determine how well I am doing at meeting their expectations?

4. How do I translate those expectations into process specifications?
5. How do I determine how well my competition is doing at meeting my customer's expectations?

GATHERING THE VOICE OF THE CUSTOMER

Now that the definitions of the terms "process" and "process management" have been discussed, where does the next step of our journey begin? The answer is: "Always begin with the customer!" Remember that the ultimate goal is improved customer satisfaction, increased business performance, along with any corresponding reduction in costs, so begin by looking at, or listening to, the customer. The fulfillment of customers' needs is accomplished through your process steps and effective process management. In order to focus on the most crucial processes, one must understand what is important to the customer.

You begin by identifying your customer expectations and prioritizing which process has the greatest impact on those expectations. Earlier we discussed using the customer impact to develop the Process Prioritization Matrix, PPM. You might identify new information in this step that would cause you to update the PPM. This review from the customer's perspective will help you prioritize these processes. For example, if a customer's feedback (in the form of complaints, results of surveys, marketing reports, customer visits, etc.) indicates that timeliness of financial statements or invoices is one of the most important issue to them, then the subprocess of "billing statement creation and distribution" or "Customer MIS report generation" might be a likely focus for further review. A primary criterion for process selection should be based on what the customer deems to be crucial.

In order to determine what is crucial to the customer, we must begin by identifying as many sources for the *Voice of the Customer* (VOC) information as possible. Review available sources such as customer satisfaction data, customer complaint logs, results of customer surveys, call monitoring records, etc. This exercise will also help you assess your VOC capabilities. Many organizations find significant gaps in the information they have been collecting and have to rethink their customer-intelligence-gathering strategies.

Here's an example: most call centers have a call quality group. This department usually makes an assessment of each Customer Service Representative's quality in handling that call. More often than not, the scoring of that information is somewhat subjective. The concept is that more professional reps lead to higher customer satisfaction. The gap you often see is that you could have the nicest rep on the phone and still not have met the customer's expectations! One recommendation we make is that when you do call monitoring, you listen to the customers as well and ask yourself what customers expect to happen when they call. Did you meet that expectation? Why or why not? It might even be possible to identify new business opportunities by listening to your customers in this way.

TRANSLATING THE VOICE OF THE CUSTOMER

Now granted, what you may hear from the customer is not always clearly an expectation. To quote Pete Pande and Larry Holpp from *What is Six Sigma?*, "This work, involving the Voice of the Customer, may be challenging. Customer themselves are often not sure about what they want or have trouble expressing it." You have to translate that voice into a meaningful and measurable expectation. Tables 3-4 and 3-5 show a few examples.

Other times the customer's stated need hides a real or more complex need. This is often the case when what you hear from your customer sounds like a solution. For example, in a technologies department, it is common to receive a work request such as adding a field to a customer record screen rather than hearing the root cause problem that the proposed solution is intended to fix. If you are to really understand the customer's need, you must look beyond their stated need.

Another situation you might face is when you have a very long list of expectations. Even with prioritization, you may face a challenge if your team has identified 150 different expectations! You could use an affinity

TABLE 3-4. Service Example

CUSTOMER EXPECTATION/REQUIREMENT	PROCESS REQUIREMENT
My card comes quickly.	Turnaround time for processing application.
No errors on the card.	Customer's name is spelled correctly.
I get a response to my inquiries and complaints.	Telephone answered fast. Problem resolved the first time.

TABLE 3-5. Manufacturing Example

CUSTOMER EXPECTATION/REQUIREMENT	PRODUCT REQUIREMENT
A good product.	Product meets the specifications in the contract.
It arrives when I need it.	On-time delivery

exercise to categorize and create higher-level categories to group these expectations. One technique you can use is to write each expectation onto a separate "sticky" note and place all of the notes on a large, erasable white board. As a team you begin to group the like terms together. Once you have approximately 5 to 10 categories, write the name for each category and a brief description explaining that category. This gives you a manageable set of categories to begin with for a high-level process.

On the other hand, you might need the original level of detail in order to truly understand your customer's needs. This is particularly applicable when you are applying these techniques to a new product or process development. In this situation you can attempt to group the expectations by product or process features. A good reference for this is the book *Managing Customer Value* by Bradley T. Gale.

UNDERSTANDING THE VOICE OF THE CUSTOMER

The final tool to discuss here is called the Kano model. This tool is valuable in understanding specific attributes of the expectations your customers have. This provides you with valuable insight into those expectations and can help you prioritize the expectations. The model is based on a structured survey tool that identifies whether a product or service feature is a specific customer expectation. The survey tool itself can be very enlightening; however, it can become fairly complex, as with most surveys.

The attributes the survey identifies are defined as:

1. Attractive Quality—These attributes of your product or service are attractive to the consumer. This is good news from a competitive standpoint, but they rarely stay as attractors. The incremental delight quickly fades as the attributes become expected by the consumer.
2. Unitary Quality—These types of attributes can cause both satisfaction and dissatisfaction.
3. Expected Quality—An expected quality dimension.

I recently checked in to one of my favorite hotels for a week of Six Sigma training I was leading. Arriving late from the airport, I checked into the hotel. My reservation was there, my frequent guest number was in the system, and the room type I had requested was available. The counter staff was very pleasant and provided me with several alternative food suggestions because I had arrived too late for dinner service. They then provided me with several coupons for the buffet breakfast.

The fact that my room was there was an example of expected quality. I expected a room because I had reserved it. If you don't get the basics right, you don't get the chance to do anything else with the customer! The fact that they did not have room service or restaurant food available that late dissatisfied me. However, they were very proactive at helping me arrange a late meal. Human service like this can provide your customer with both a great and a poor experience. This is an example of unitary quality, a quality attribute that can lead to both positive and negative experiences. The food coupons, like frequent flyer upgrades, are examples of attractive quality. You quickly come to expect them and even become disappointed if they are absent. Companies that compete only by trying to have the latest gadget or program will eventually fail if they do not deliver on the expected quality dimension.

MEASURING THE VOICE OF THE CUSTOMER

The question we are facing at this point is how to determine how well we are meeting those customer expectations. We need a way to see if our existing metrics that were identified in the Define Phase do this for us. The tool that is most commonly used is the Quality Function Deployment Matrix (QFD), which is also known as the house of quality. This is a highly flexible tool commonly used with Lean Six Sigma projects that can also be used with Six Sigma Process Management.

Figure 3-5 is a simplified view of the standard QFD. Each numbered area is called a room in the house and has a specific function. Room 1 is where you put your customer's expectations and their importance ranking, Room 2 is for benchmarking, Room 3 is where you put your metrics (House 1 only), Room 4 is where you analyze the relationships that give you the score at the bottom, and Room 5 records interactions among your metrics.

Figure 3-6 shows an example for a new paper development process. Notice that we have our customer's expectations on the left and our measures of success on the top. Sometimes practitioners refer to Room 1 as "The Whats" and Room 2 as "The Hows."

Based on this example, smoothness is the most crucial metric because it has the most impact on the customer expectations. You can see this from

FIGURE 3-5.

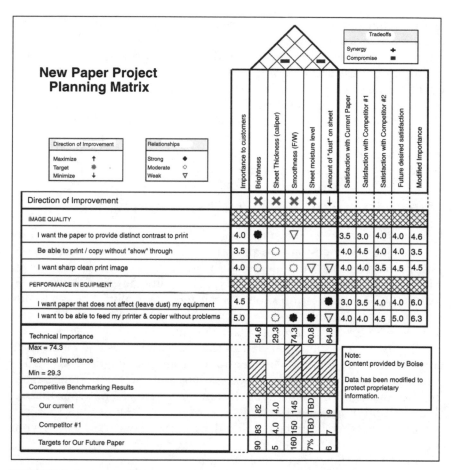

FIGURE 3-6. *Courtesy of International TechneGroup Incorporated http://www.qfdcapture.com*

the scoring line that is titled technical importance on the bottom. This is the most common scoring method and is called the "Technical Standard Score." In this method, you assign the value of 9, 3, 1, or 0 in the relationship cell for each combination of metric and expectation. Nine means there is a strong relationship, 3 a moderate one, 1 is weak, and 0 means no relationship at all. You then would weight each score by the importance ranking for the expectation before totaling that column.

This tool can become very complicated very quickly if the scope is not carefully managed. It will do you no good to try to make sense from a QFD that contains a matrix of 100 columns by 100 rows! Once again, this is a living tool that will be updated again in the Measure phase as additional metrics are identified. There are several valuable techniques for maintaining the scope at a manageable level. One of the most common is to try to keep it to the level of your view. What this means is if I am building a QFD for a high-level, end-to-end process, I should only include expectations and metrics that match that end-to-end level. I would then sort out those that are relevant only to a specific process step and place them on a separate QFD.

Often the QFD will help you validate where you are missing a needed metric or where you have a metric that is not needed. This is seen by blank rows or blank columns. If you have a customer's expectation, a row, that has no relationship score on it, then you have no measures for that expectation. If this is a valid expectation, in this case a new metric will be needed. The other scenario is when you have a metric, a column, that has no score in it. This means that this specific metric has no relationship to any of the customer's expectations. It might be a valuable business measure, such as a productivity indicator, but has little or no bearing on the customer.

LINKING THE CUSTOMER TO THE PROCESS

Determining the customer expectations and the corresponding process requirement is an easy concept to comprehend, but it is often harder to develop in real practice. Obtaining the information that you need to develop these requirements is challenging. One place to start is to return to the Process Prioritization Matrix developed earlier. Ask yourself the following questions:

1. What are the top two or three most crucial processes listed in the matrix?
2. How did they score in the areas of customer impact?
3. What information sources were used in order to determine those scores?

Now use this data to determine which of your high-level business processes has the strongest impact on your "Voice of the Customer," and focus your improvement efforts there. You can then use a simple criteria matrix to help understand and prioritize the processes that most impact the customer's experience (see Table 3-6).

Once again, the more advanced tool that can be used here is the Quality Function Deployment Matrix (QFD). A common strategy is to create a multiple-level QFD. Once again, this can be simple and practical, or it can become complex and cumbersome. What you do is take the crucial metrics you prioritized off the top of your previous QFD, we will call that House 1, and place them on the left-hand side of your new QFD, which we will call House 2. In place of the measures you had before on the top (room 3), you would now list your process steps. This allows you to use the QFD matrix to prioritize your process activity. Think of it this way. House 1 allows you to link your key customer metrics to your

TABLE 3-6.

CUSTOMER REQUIREMENTS	PROCESS			
	PURCHASING	SPECIFICATION AND BID	DISTRIBUTION	CREDIT AND COLLECTION
Accurate billing	1	1		1
On-time delivery		1	1	
Flexible requirements	1	1		
Total	2	3	1	1

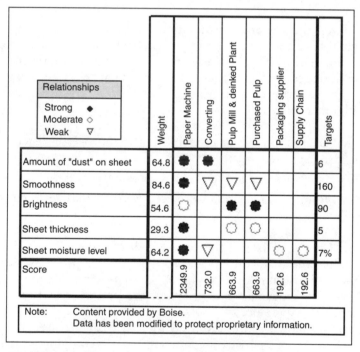

FIGURE 3-7. *Courtesy of International TechneGroup Incorporated*
http://www.qfdcapture.com

customer's expectations, and House 2 allows you to extend that link to your processes (see Figure 3-7).

Once you see how this linking works, you can continue to link down many levels. One example would be to then link your processes to the next level of functions and so on. You are also not limited to just this structure. The QFD is a very flexible facilitation tool we often use for team-based decision making.

DEVELOPING CUSTOMER METRICS

This is where you begin to use the output from the previous QFD exercise. The QFD helped you determine which metrics have the greatest impact on the customer's expectations. In the Define phase you were primarily looking at what metrics we have now that are customer focused, with one eye on what new metrics we should have. Later, in the Measure phase, you will see where we will again look for potential new metrics that might be needed. Also, you will actually begin to build and test these measures later in the Analyze phase.

If new measures have been identified, you will need to begin data collection to evaluate their performance. This means you must determine performance standards that meet the customer's expectations. We talk at length in the Analyze section on how to set those standards. You will need to understand some details about the data you will begin to collect in order to be able to set those standards. In order to prepare you for that, we have listed some of the typical attributes of metrics those standards will be based on.

Data sources—Where will the data come from that will be used to establish the metrics? Who owns the data? Will you need funding to create MIS reports?

Measurement type—Is it discrete data (such as yes or no) or is it a continuous data (such as average thickness.) How is the data measured? If it is a physical measurement, how is it collected? If a logical measurement, such as Call Handle Time, where does the measurement begin and end? What is included in the measurement?

QUICK DEFINITION ▬▬▬▬▬▬▬▬▬▬▬▬▬▬▬▬▬▬▬▬▬

Discrete data is data that can be characterized as yes/no, on/off or a specific discrete value.

QUICK DEFINITION ▬▬▬▬▬▬▬▬▬▬▬▬▬▬▬▬▬▬▬▬▬

Continuous data is data that can be characterized as having any value over a range of numbers.

Upper and/or Lower Limits—If it is continuous data, at what point is it too short or too long, too early or too late, etc. If it is discrete, what specifications are there for this metric? How were they set and who is responsible for setting them?

Later we will look at how to define defects in comparison to these specifications. At this point you will need to be aware and if possible begin to evaluate your performance in each of these metrics. Later we will discuss the concepts of Capability, Throughput, and Sigma levels.

COMPARING THE COMPETITION'S PERFORMANCE

Much has been written about Benchmarking since a famous book by that name was published by ASQ press in 1989. And quite honestly, even though much is written each year, there is still very little new to say about it! We have listed some resources for you in the back of the book for further detail. What is important is how you go about linking any competitive information to your customers' expectations and metrics. For every one of the expectations you've identified in the previous QFD, you should also try to identify how well your competitors are performing in the eyes of your customers. For example, if you produce specialized semiconductor chips for consumer applications, one of your customer's expectations might be first-pass accuracy for product qualification tests. How well are your competitors doing at this? Is that dimension strategically important to your company? If so you might rank that expectation higher.

There are two ways to display competition on your QFD table. The most common is to add a room off to the right of the main matrix in the center of the QFD. This is shown as room 2 in the previous graphic. You can either use a numerical score or a simple text comparison such as better, same, or worse.

One recent adaptation to the QFD has been to add a room at the bottom of the matrix that links competitive scores to the metrics on the top. In many industries you have trade publications or public customer satisfaction surveys that repeatedly report your and your competitor's performance against an expectation with a standard measure. For example, U.S. commercial airlines monthly on-time departure percentages and other relevant flight statistics are widely published and available. Many statistics are gathered by governmental agencies such as the Department of Transportation and are housed on the Web. It might also be found in a *Consumer Reports* magazine or J.D. Powers survey.

While the primary purpose for Six Sigma Process Management is to create an effective process management system, it is useful to know that the same tools you are using to gain process knowledge will also help you understand your performance against competition.

DEFINE PHASE SUMMARY

This phase represents a combination of both Lean Six Sigma and Project management tools that help you initiate effort and begin to develop your process management system. In this phase you define the scope of your project, gather and align resources, and begin to understand your process from the customer's point of view. The customer's expectations become the launching point for everything else we do. We call this the "Voice of the Customer," and it will drive everything whether it is defining metrics, establishing process performance, or identifying crucial failures.

DEFINE PHASE CHECKLIST

- [ ] Has the appropriate level of sponsorship been given to the team?
- [ ] Is the team comprised of the correct representatives?
- [ ] Has the Leadership team defined the core (highest-level) processes?
- [ ] Has a process been selected for Six Sigma Process Management?
- [ ] Have you identified your customer's expectations for the product or service delivered by that process?
- [ ] Have you used the Kano survey or other tool to rank your customer's expectations?
- [ ] Have you identified the existing metrics for that process?
- [ ] Have you used the QFD or another prioritization tool to evaluate whether your measurement system adequately links to your metrics?
- [ ] Do you know your current performance for those metrics?
- [ ] Do you know your competitor's performance relative to the customer's perception?

DEFINE PHASE TOOLS

Six Sigma Process Management Project Charter
Process Decomposition Chart
SIPOC Diagram

QFD
Focus Groups
Surveys
Customer Affinity Diagrams
Complaint Research
Benchmarking

THE MEASURE PHASE

Objective Statement: The objective of the Measure phase is to create detailed diagrams of your process, collect and validate existing data, and build any new metrics needed.

Structure: There are two main sections to the Measure phase: Documenting the Process and Measuring the Process.

DOCUMENTING THE PROCESS

Key questions to answer:

1. How do I map a process?
2. What should be included in the map?
3. When should I use what type of map?
4. What type of data should I put on the map?

PROCESS DOCUMENTATION STANDARDS

There are many different standards for documenting your process flow. We will show the two most prominent in today's quality environment. We encourage you to be flexible and creative in how you apply these tools or some combination of them. People might argue that one is better than the other; however, our belief is that each has an appropriate application in continuous process improvement.

There are several side benefits you will encounter from the mapping process. In order to correctly map a process, you should "Walk the Process" in order to see it for yourself. This often leads to discovery of bottlenecks, redundancy, or waste! In order to ensure that you have correctly captured everything, you should always review your results with a subject matter expert before you finalize process documentation.

PROCESS FLOWCHARTING METHOD

The process flowchart model most Six Sigma practitioners use begins with a high-level map called a level-1 map. A level-1 map describes the top five to seven steps in a process without decision boxes or alternative paths. Often there is a more detailed verbal description shown below each box on it. You can also utilize the SIPOC diagram that was shown in the Define phase as your level-1 map. Figure 3-8 has an example of a level-1 map from American Express that was presented at an HMBA Six Sigma in Financial Services conference.

Notice that the area of focus was determined to be the premium serving area. In this example the Master Black Belt then continued to decompose the model into successively lower levels of documentation. As you drill down, you add more detailed information. You would select the area of focus from the level-1 map and begin to expand that into level 2. In level 2 you would begin to add swim lanes, which are horizontal lines that separate different business units or departments and include your process documentation (see Figure 3-9).

At this point you have a decision to make. You can either focus on a small portion of the process to document, or carry the detail down to the next level for the entire process. Typically, you would only need to go down to level 3 for a Black Belt project. For your Six Sigma Process Management initiative, it would not be necessary to acquire this level of detail yet. In the example above, each of the two pinpointed areas would be potential measurement points and would identify areas for improvement projects. In the next level down, the Black Belt would focus on detailing the specific steps in each of those circled process steps.

One common problem companies experience is how much should be mapped. We have seen several examples of companies who have engaged in endless mapping exercises without a clue as to what to do with the information. This will continue to be a concern due to the recent arrival of Sarbanes-Oxley and its focus on processes. While it is refreshing to see this renewed focus on process that has been unprecedented in the financial and accounting fields, many are unsure as to what to do with the information or question whether it helps them. If the linkage to process improvement activities and savings are not quickly pointed out, then this initiative will wither.

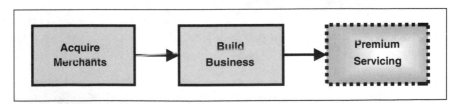

FIGURE 3-8.

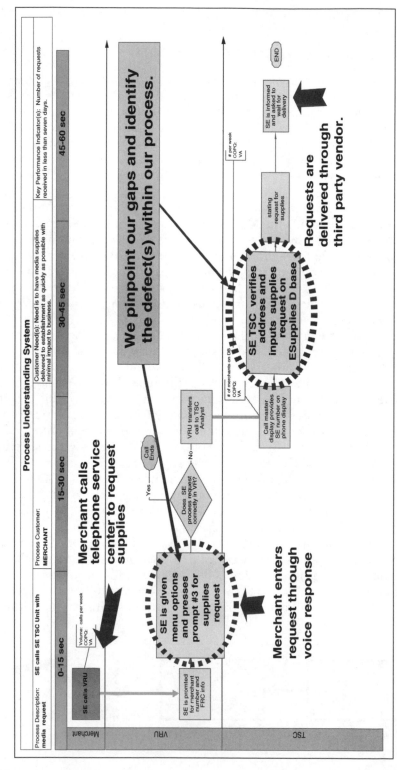

FIGURE 3-9. Level 2 process map.

64

DOCUMENTING YOUR MAP

The process map can be a very versatile tool. One of the most frequent uses is as a documentation tool. This helps keep your maps live, versus stored on a bookshelf or a file cabinet somewhere.

Documenting the costs of the process will help you identify the cost of poor quality (COPQ). As you walk through the process, collect as much information as possible about the process, even if it is just documentation as to what data is available and the data sources. Look for information sources for volume, costs, rework, and staffing as a start.

Examples of types of details that can be documented on the map are:

- Cycle time
- Volume and Flow data
- People or work areas
- Defect information
- Relevant cost information

By documenting these types of process details on your map, it becomes a living tool for managing your process. These critical process characteristics will form the basis for your measurement and process improvement targets.

Later, as we use these maps to identify process failures, you will use this information to calculate the cost of poor quality and the impact of those failures. Also, as you establish ongoing performance metrics, you will already have your data sources identified.

VALUE STREAM MAPPING METHOD

Another variation of mapping that has evolved from the Lean and Lean Six Sigma fields is called Value Stream mapping. Lean has a strong emphasis on waste and inventory reduction driving process efficiency as compared to Six Sigma's focus on reducing variation and defects for quality improvement.

While the Process Flowchart focuses on trying to identify all the activities in a specific process, the Value Stream Map does this for a specific product or product family (see Figure 3-10).

This level of focus works very well for a specific type of transaction in a service or a product in a manufacturing plant. Another diagram that is often used in conjunction with a Value Stream Map is a Time Line Map. This map graphically displays the value and non-value-added time steps proportionately along a time line. Following is an example presented by Bank of America at a recent conference (see Figure 3-11).

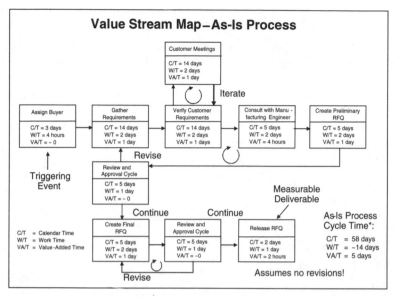

FIGURE 3-10. *Courtesy Liz Keim, Managing Partner Integrated Quality Resources, LLC*

USING YOUR MAPS

As a final note on process mapping, if your company is ISO certified, you should always cross-reference your maps against your ISO documentation. The appropriate procedure manuals should clearly define the expected process behavior and will provide a good reference source for process information as well. The limitation is that the documentation is often focused on a process task and not on the process itself. You can check what you have documented as the actual, or as-is, process against the planned process. The analysis of the gaps will provide additional valuable information for process improvement. Often, quick gains can be made by reinforcing what should be happening. This might also show you a crucial measurement point. Once the process management system is established, your scorecard might direct you back to this point to redesign this process. Do not accept the expected process in the current ISO documentation as the "should be" process until you are sure that this process is capable of meeting the customer's expectations. We cover how to measure process capability later in this chapter.

MEASURING THE PROCESS

Key questions to answer:

1. What data should I collect?

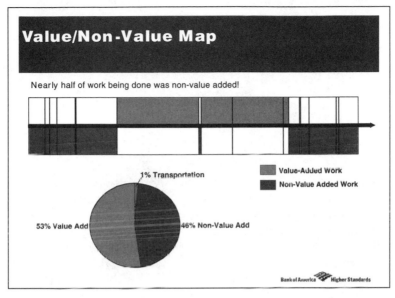

FIGURE 3-11.

2. What is a process management metric?
3. How do I decide where to install new customer metrics?
4. How do I validate my metrics?

COLLECT EXISTING MEASURES

Just to refresh your memory, back in the Define phase we began to identify existing measures and potential new measures. Now that we have a better understanding of our processes, we need to focus more on identifying new metrics. You begin by looking through satisfaction survey data, customer service complaint data, and any other documentation, such as customer letters and e-mails. If you have customer complaint data, review it to determine the highest number of recurring complaints. Attempt to categorize reasons for repeat customer calls. Monitoring customer calls is also an effective tool for understanding the function being reviewed. Remember that most current call monitoring focuses on the call representative performance. Also link back to the previously identified process maps to see if you can determine what the customer is trying to tell you about the process. What attribute of the process is the customer dissatisfied with? Is it the cycle time or the accuracy of a process step? Are there other reasons for dissatisfaction? Verify that you have captured any expectations on your QFD.

At this point you should be asking how what you're doing here is different than what we began in the Define phase. In the Define phase, you were more focused on high-level metrics. These are the measures directly

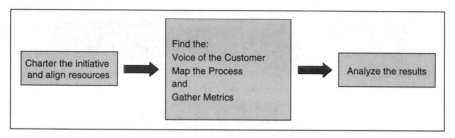

FIGURE 3-12.

tied to your customer's expectations. In Six Sigma jargon, we often call these high-level metrics the Critical to Customer Ys. Now you are able to focus on a more detailed extension of what you began before because now you have the process mapping completed. Another crucial difference is that you will drill deeper into your processes to find lower-level metrics.

Once again, as you begin to get a hang of the flow of these phases, you will realize that many of these activities can be conducted concurrently, thus saving you a tremendous amount of cycle time!

Figure 3-12 is a model of the flow without the Six Sigma phase structure.

The one tool that brings it all back together is the QFD that we looked at before. The QFD can be used in two ways here, often described as two levels. Level one aligns your Customer Requirements (VOC) to your metrics. This helps prioritize which metrics measure what is most important to the customer. Level two helps you align those most important metrics to your processes, meaning which process (or process step) has the most impact on your customer!

IDENTIFY POTENTIAL NEW MEASURES

Okay, you already know how to focus on the most crucial customer requirements; now you have to decide how best to measure them. Let's use the prior table of expectations and process requirements found in the Define phase. Here are some examples of metrics identified by listening to the Voice of the Customer (see Table 3-7).

This is not the only opportunity you have to identify new metrics. Later, in the Analyze phase, you will have one more chance to identify potential measures once you have completed the failure identification exercise.

IDENTIFY DATA SOURCES

Often you will find that data does not exist for a specific expectation to be measured. Once you have identified what you want to measure, you have to plan how you want to collect it. A data collection plan is a structured

Table 3-7.

Service Example		
Customer Requirement	Process Requirement	Voice of the Customer Metric
My card comes quickly	Turnaround time for processing an application	Cycle time for application processing Approvals within 24 hours of receipt
No errors on the card	Customer's information is correct	Number of replacement cards due to misspelled names Number of replacement cards due to incorrect company name
I get a response to my inquiries and complaints	First-time problem resolution	Number of times a customer called two or more times for the same issue.

Table 3-8.

Proposed Metric	
Metric Name	Name of New Proposed Measure
Metric Definition	A definition that is sufficiently complete enough to allow users to understand purpose of measure
Process Area	What area or process step is being measured?
Metric Owner	Who is responsible for collecting and reporting this measure?
Data Source	What is the source file origination for the data?
Frequency	Is it to be collected hourly, weekly or monthly?
Sampling	Is it collected by sampling or from a total population?
Benefit	High-level benefits that collecting this data will provide.

plan designed to help facilitate this process. This plan should outline basic pieces of information that is needed for each type of source data. Table 3-8 is an example.

We foreshadowed the need for this in the Define phase. The final element to consider in collecting data is whether it will be based on a sample of the data. There are many good references on sampling techniques for data.

The key concept to remember is that a good sample is not based on a percentage or size of the file. A good sample is determined based on variability of the data or the potential for error within the data.

VALIDATE YOUR DATA

Data validation is the step where you verify that the data you are using to create your measures actually means what you think it does. A common example is data that has been collected by human operators. This data is subject to interpretation or misunderstanding. Additionally, any manually collected, coded data is an opportunity for an incorrect code to be applied. One company I recently met with had 253 separate and distinct codes for a call representative to use just to explain why a goodwill adjustment was necessary.

Automated data collection is also subject to misinterpretation. A common example is statistics that are calculated by Automated Call Director (ACD) phone systems. Make sure you clearly know where the measurement begins and where it ends. How are transferred calls tracked in the handle-time statistics?

The entire category of data testing methods is called Measurement Systems Analysis. While there are volumes that speak to statistical methods of testing, we would like to alert you to the two most common. In the back of the book you will find recommendations for further instruction.

The first method of data validation you need to be aware of is called a Gage R&R. The R&R stands for repeatability and reproducibility. It is a statistical testing procedure to calculate the percentage of time that each operator correctly repeats the same measurement, and each group of operators reproduces the same measurement given the same opportunity. There are two types of Gage R&R studies, one for continuous data and one for discrete. An example of a continuous study would be when you have an inspector measuring a mechanical part size. The measurement dimensions represent a continuous data type. You would use a gage R&R study to ensure that any variation in measurement comes from the parts, not from the inspector or the inspection tool.

Discrete or attribute measures are commonly found in data that can be described as "yes/no," "good/bad," or "high/medium/low." In these examples, your inspector is commonly working to a standard for the particular attribute they are measuring and providing a determination code for that attribute. It could also be the example previously given where there are 253 discrete codes!

The other method we recommend is a measurement systems review. With this method you are verifying the data collection process and system definitions in an automated data system. It is helpful here to actually map the flow of the data just as you did with the process and identify where and when it is collected and any calculations applied to the data.

In the situation where there is manual data intervention, it is usually pretty obvious to most that error could creep into the reported measurements. It is in the automated scenario (where there is the implicit assumption that the data is correct because the data collection is automated) that you will have to challenge people's perceptions. One recent example in a large company revealed that one department was collecting the data on an excel spreadsheet then uploading to the company's accounting system because that geographic location could not afford the automated interface device for data collection. Their interpretation of what was correct led to the entire report being invalid for that department.

The philosophy in data validation is no different than the old adage, "Measure twice; cut once." The intent being to validate your data (measurements) before changing the process.

SURROGATE MEASURES

One final point on measurement is what to do when it is impractical to create the metric you need. This can happen for many reasons, such as lack of technology in certain process areas or due to the cost of collection. In these situations you may have to identify what are called surrogate measures. These are measures that would not be your first choice but do have some direct relationship to your customer. While not precise, they can help you track directional trends.

MEASURE PHASE SUMMARY

The overall DMA process can be seen as a series of steps drilling deeper downward while developing knowledge. You have documented your processes, gathered and validated available measures, and proposed new ones. Now you have created your process maps and are staring at a large amount of information, much of which you never knew before about your process. Now let's talk about what to do with all of it!

MEASURE PHASE CHECKLIST

☐ Have you identified your critical customer requirements?
☐ Have you prioritized which process area has the greatest impact on those requirements?

☐ Have you mapped those processes?

☐ Have you identified existing metrics and determined which ones are relevant?

☐ Have you identified new metrics based on the gaps identified with the QFD?

☐ Have you validated that the data used to create these measures is valid?

MEASURE PHASE TOOLS

QFD
Value Stream Maps
Flow Charts
Sampling
Measurement Systems Review
Gage R&R
Regression analysis
Process Capability
Sigma values

THE ANALYZE PHASE

Objective Statement: The objective of the Analyze phase is to understand the performance of your current process, the key drivers of that perform-ance, and to identify the common failures in that process. This allows you to establish effective performance standards for process performance. *Okay, so this is the technical section!*

Structure: There are three main sections in the Analyze phase: Under-standing Process Relationships, Establishing Baseline Standards, and Identifying Process Failures.

UNDERSTANDING PROCESS RELATIONSHIPS

Key question to answer:

1. How do I ensure that my metrics are really the key drivers of customer satisfaction?

Y=F(X) MEANS BUILDING
LINKS IN YOUR METRICS

This step of linking your metrics together is often overlooked in the process of building a Six Sigma Process Management system. In the previous steps, you began to link your metrics to the customer's expectations using the QFD. You then began to identify lower-level metrics within your process map. The question then becomes how do I know which metric is the best to use? You will also notice that some are very detailed and some are more comprehensive. What is needed is a structure that will allow you to organize your measures in a meaningful and useful way. This is called linking your Ys and Xs. Your Ys are the internal measures closest to the customer, while your Xs are the internal measures closest to your processes.

There are two visual ways to describe the structure of the measures you are creating; they are upstream/downstream or hierarchical. Think of a stream in the woods, and no this is not a relaxation technique! If you know what the speed of the water is upstream and the key widths through the river that may cause the water to speed up or slow down, then you can predict the speed downstream. In your business processes, if you know the process performance upstream, than you might be able to predict the resulting performance downstream. In the transactional business world, some have called this in-process and results measures.

This concept is slightly different than the throughput metrics used in manufacturing. In throughput you are combining the performance of the in-process measures (yields) to determine the total process performance (yield). Another way to look at it is that throughput is a horizontal measurement view, whereas your hierarchical process structure is a more vertical view. Here we are looking at the relationships that one or more measures might have on the result of the overall process measures. For example, our QFD might have identified a customer expectation to be a timely arrival of their shipment. We measured this as "cycle time of product delivered within 24 hours of request." In looking at the product ordering process during the mapping exercise, we identified potential upstream process measures such as "positive credit check score" or "stock outs." We believe that these are drivers of our product not being delivered in a timely fashion.

REGRESSION ANALYSIS

Once you begin to collect the data, you can then statistically test the validity of your assumptions of linkage using regression analysis, logistic regression, or other similar analytical techniques.

In the following graphs we tested both to see if they were drivers of cycle time. In the first graph it is easy to see that "stock outs" were not a good predictor of delayed cycle time. (See Figure 3-13.)

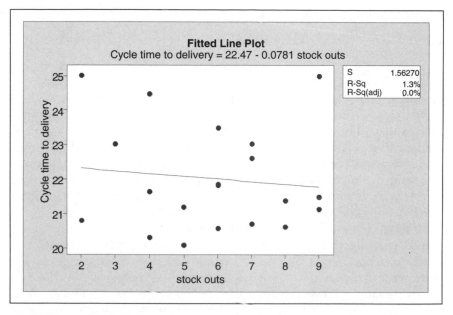

FIGURE 3-13.

In the next test for credit check score, we saw a more positive result (see Figure 3-14).

In this example we have determined that "credit check score" is an upstream measure that is a good predictor of performance in our product delivery. As a side note, this does not mean that "Stock Outs" is not a valuable metric to our process management system. "Stock Outs" in itself might be a separate Y with its own drivers, or it might be an upstream measure to a different downstream measure! Investigate further before throwing the baby out with the bath water.

THE HIERARCHY OF MEASUREMENT

This last example by all means was intended to provide a simplistic view for a simple linear relationship. In our previous mapping exercise, we talked about mapping down multiple levels (three or more) in a process. We could conceivably have measures at each level that are related. The visual structure that describes this is a hierarchical structure (see Figure 3-15).

You could create a series of measures that link based on the process level you are viewing them at. The benefit of this structure is it allows you to create your process reporting to match the visibility of the leadership at that level. The Vice President of raw material procurement for a chemical processing plant might have a dashboard of three to five high-level, customer-focused quality measures in addition to his business and employee

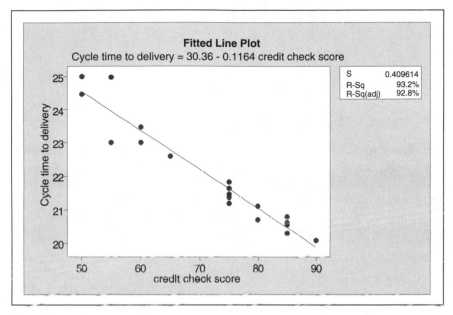

FIGURE 3-14.

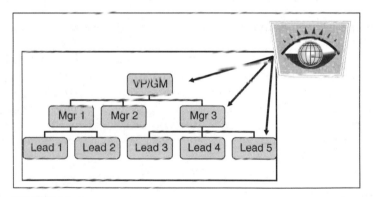

FIGURE 3-15.

measures. Her management team might each have their own process measures based on their line of sight within the process. Each of these measures should be linked and tested to ensure what they are driving. This same hierarchy can continue on down through the process levels. The hierarchy of measures should match the hierarchy of process determined in the Define phase earlier. A common hypothesis testing tool ANOVA, Analysis of Variance, is often used at this point to test the relationship between multiple low-level factors against a high-level factor. Based on the significance of the results from the ANOVA, you can use what is called a General Linear Model (GLM) to develop a predictive model.

ESTABLISH PERFORMANCE STANDARDS

Key question to answer:

How do I establish performance goals for my measures?

ESTABLISH BASELINE PERFORMANCE

A business associate used to say nothing is good or bad except by comparison. Well okay, I can think of some things, however, in today's business world where we need to establish a standard for comparison of our performance in order to determine how we are doing. Are we good or bad? The purpose of this step in the analyze phase is to do just that—establish the baseline performance so we can understand how well we are doing.

QUICK DEFINITION

Baseline is the current performance level you are starting from.

In order to establish the baseline performance, we should understand some basics about our data. Evaluate how well the metrics have been performing. If it is a new metric, you might have to wait while you collect data going forward in order to establish your current baseline performance. Combine this information with the specific metric information identified in the data collection step of the Measure phase. As you look at your current performance, it is inevitable that you will begin to understand why the data is performing at the current level. This is the crucial linkage to projects from process.

PROCESS CAPABILITY

As you begin to understand more about the performance of the metric, you can begin to analyze what is called the capability of the process. In order to do that we must again look back to our Voice of the Customer information, because of course everything begins and ends with the customer! What was their expectation for service delivery or product conformance?

QUICK DEFINITION

Capability is the ability of your process to meet the customer's requirements.

Capability is defined as the ability of the product or service to meet the customers' requirements. Using the visual metaphor of a pair of football goalposts representing the standard you must achieve to meet your customer' requirements, what percentage of the time do you kick the ball between the posts to score? When you do kick it through, how close was it to one of the posts? In Lean Six Sigma we measure that process capability in terms of sigma levels. This allows us to statistically understand the probability of your process meeting the expectations of your customers. This is the probability of being in between the goalposts!

This is often represented by the process capability formula: Cp = Specification width/Process capability, where specification is your customer's requirements and capability is the observed variability in your product or process ability to achieve that requirement. You achieve Six Sigma when the chances of not meeting the specifications are equal to or less than 3.4 times out of every 1 million opportunities. In other words, it's pretty darn small!

With the inclusion of Lean techniques into the Six Sigma lexicon, the classical definition of a defect also broadened. The additional concept here that needs to be called out is the concept of waste as a defect. Up till now most of our examples have been using a customer standard such as cycle time to define our defect. The concept of waste is broadly defined as any activity that requires resources (time, money, labor, etc.) but does not provide value. In a manufacturing facility, it is usually easy to see waste in the form of excess inventory, scrap, unnecessary transportation time, or rework queues. In a service center, you might find rework in the form of an escalation desk in a call center or repeat visits to a client's installation.

DEVELOP PERFORMANCE GOALS

This is where we establish the performance goals for the metrics you have identified. First we needed to understand what the customer expected, and we had to link that expectation to our process. Second we needed to understand how capable we are of meeting those expectations. Now we can finally set performance goals. The reason we needed to know the capability first is that the process might be, and often is, incapable of meeting the customer's expectations. In that case the simple act of setting higher goals will not increase your ability to meet those goals. You must change the process! Motivation will never overcome a poor process design on an ongoing basis.

Now that we've gotten that off our chests, let's talk about how to use this knowledge. You can begin to analyze the trade-offs between percent improvements, the customer impact, and the cost of change. In the next section we begin to discuss where to introduce change into your processes.

FINALIZE THE METRICS

On a final note, you can now begin to build the metrics you have previously identified and tested. You should have all the information you need to create the reports and begin data collection at this point. One frequent concern is the cost of developing these metrics, and there are two crucial points that need to be made. First is that your measures and goals will change over time, requiring you to be flexible. The lower-level or in-process metrics will change more rapidly than the high-level ones.

Second, remember to balance your process management activities with your improvement activities so that the development of your Six Sigma Process Management system is self-funding! Remember (yet again!) that the purpose of all these efforts is to help you determine where to focus your improvement efforts. This ties back to our Define phase when we worked to identify which process we wanted to focus on first. Most Lean Six Sigma programs begin with only running projects that are great for addressing the easy and quick changes. If you identify the process area you want to begin with and initiate a few simple projects on known defects, you can use the savings generated by those efforts to fund the development of the data collection processes needed. This becomes an iterative process as you progress through your organization.

PROCESS FAILURES

Key questions to answer:

How do I determine where my process fails?

FAILURE POINT IDENTIFICATION

Remember that the purpose of all these efforts up till now is to help you determine where to focus your improvement efforts. (Have we said this before?) Up to this point, your effort has been to create a scorecard of metrics to best measure your processes, document your processes, validate the linkages, and assess their capability. Along the way you have undoubtedly heard many tales of woe as to what the problems were and written them down. Now we begin to explore in a more systematic way where these processes fail. The first step we call slamming the Voice of the Customer into the Voice of the Process. Once again the QFD can help us with this process. This was what we did in building the house 2 of the QFD.

SLAMMING THE CUSTOMER INTO THE PROCESS

The purpose of this exercise is to lead us to where in our business we have the greatest impact on the customer. The next step is to look into that area to see what metrics we have established. Have we quantitatively linked those metrics to the big Ys of the customer? If so, we can further focus our efforts down to where we have those lower-level metrics. Now we need an exercise to help uncover the types of failure that can occur in these processes. We do this using a two-step workshop exercise.

Step 1. The VOC Slam. In this exercise you need a large-scale version of your detailed process map to work from. Often we project the image of the process map onto a white board that you can then draw on with an erasable marker or use sticky notes to document where the failures occur. Then gather the team together and begin to identify where in the process you fail to meet the customer's expectations. The risk here is that the team will migrate to the "failure du jour!" This means that the most recent pain will normally get the most attention. You should do this quantitatively by including your customer complaint information. Make sure you keep everyone focused on the customer. Keep repetitively going back to your customer's expectations and asking the team, "How did we not meet this expectation?" Followed by, "Why did that happen?" This exercise has the team continuously drilling down into the process. This exercise will create a large number of potential problems to analyze. Many of these problems will be insignificant, but many will be valuable nuggets. It is similar to the old style of mineral mining where they would fire a high-pressure stream of water at the side of a hill and then filter through the mud runoff for the few nuggets that would appear! While this exercise has always been wildly successful in generating multiple ideas, many teams often fall short in following up on analyzing the output for projects.

Step 2. The Cleanup. Once you have gone through Step 1 and exhausted all of your VOC information, you then have them walk step-by-step through the process to identify what could go wrong that could impact the customer. You want to make sure you do this task second because the team will naturally gravitate to the known problems that concern or affect them, not necessarily what is important to the customer. Step 1 keeps them focused on the customer.

This activity will complete the Define/Measure/Analyze phase of Six Sigma Process Management. The last activity to do here is to actually walk through the process with your new process knowledge. Can you visually see your process management system as you walk through the process? When you look at work steps, you start to see the ways to measure and link the impacts to your customer! You see how the failures occur and where! Now we need to discuss where to go next in order to take your business to the next level.

ANALYZE PHASE SUMMARY

In the analyze phase we linked our metrics together into a process hierarchy that visually made sense and described our process. We tested those metrics so that we could quantitatively describe the process using fairly simple modeling techniques. We then beat up the process to identify the failures within the process that most impacted our customers.

ANALYZE PHASE CHECKLIST

☐ Can you quantitatively link them to the high-quality metrics previously defined?
☐ Is the process capable?
☐ Where does it fail?
☐ Can you see where the failures occur in the process map?

ANALYZE TOOLS

Regression analysis
ANOVA analysis
Pareto Charts
Performance charts and graphs

SUCCESSFULLY MANAGING YOUR END-TO-END PROCESS(ES)

Up until now we have focused our attention on the crucial components for *successfully introducing* and *initially establishing* Six Sigma Process Management. In this chapter we turn our attention to the crucial components that the Process Leadership Team will use to successfully maximize the performance of their end-to-end core process(es) *on an ongoing basis*.

Specifically, we will focus on three key areas:

1. Managing a portfolio of projects across the end-to-end process;
2. Using process dashboards and scorecards;
3. Establishing cross-functional accountabilities and behaviors.

To relate these Process Leadership Team responsibilities back to our DMAIC framework, we can think of (1) above as the crucial component within the Improve phase of our Six Sigma Process Management approach, with (2) and (3) being key components of the Control phase. Before we discuss these three key areas, let's take some time to explore what we mean by *Process Governance*.

EXPLORING PROCESS GOVERNANCE

As we described in Chapter 2, the role of the Process Leadership Team is not fixed throughout your Six Sigma Process Management initiative. It changes and evolves over time.

Initially the Process Leadership Team's role is to introduce and establish the crucial Six Sigma Process Management components (described in the previous chapter). As these crucial components such as process dashboards and measurement systems are established, the Process Leadership Team's focus will increasingly evolve to one of *"process governance"*—using the Six Sigma Process Management infrastructure to successfully manage and improve their process(es)!

What specifically do we mean by *"process governance?"* Perhaps a good way to start to answer this question is to revisit our simple process diagram from Chapter 1 (see Figure 4-1). As you look at this process again, ask yourself a single, thought-provoking question: "If the CEO of my company appointed me as the end-to-end Process Owner for this process, what would I need to successfully manage it?"

As an experienced business leader, you've probably managed a number of departments and functional areas during your career. You might even have managed business processes! So, as you reflect on your overall management experience, take a few minutes to brainstorm and jot down the answer to the above question in the space provided on the next page. See if you can come up with at least eight things that you would need.

How did you do? Did you come up with eight—maybe less, maybe more? Now take a minute to review your list and highlight those items that you *don't* use to manage today—in other words the things that might be completely new in order to manage your end-to-end process. How much of your list falls into this category—two things, three, four—maybe more?

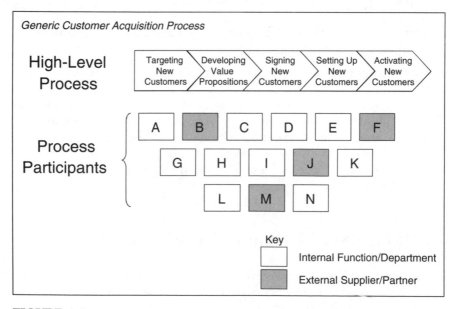

FIGURE 4-1.

**WHAT I NEED TO SUCCESSFULLY MANAGE
AN END-TO-END PROCESS**

1.

2.

3.

4.

5.

6.

7.

8.

FACING UP TO TRANSITION CHALLENGES

The reason we asked you to perform this little exercise is to illustrate a simple point. We have found that, in general, when we ask this question of business leaders, most people list very few things that are actually different than those that they require to successfully manage a department or a function.

This really shouldn't surprise us. After all, as leaders managing a department or, indeed, a process, we need to understand a number of basic things—such as how work activities get performed and who does them; we need data and information to quantify performance; we need to set goals and establish accountabilities so that we can recognize and reward performance; we need to motivate people and foster an environment that strives for continuous improvement and success; we need to deploy people to the highest priorities, and so on.

The challenge—and of course, the big difference—is that in our process world, we need to understand these things from an end-to-end process perspective as opposed to our traditional function-by-function view of the world. At times, obtaining an understanding of the things we have just listed can be particularly frustrating because many of our information systems and performance management systems have been set up to mirror our operating constructs and procedures—i.e., function by function.

It's particularly important that we continually recognize and address these challenges throughout the implementation of Six Sigma Process Management—in particular as the Process Leadership Team transitions from its role of setting up the Six Sigma Process Management infrastructure to actually using it to make better-informed, process-oriented decisions. This transition period can be a particularly challenging time for leaders and organizations that have little process management experience. Their patience and tolerance for ambiguity can be tested. "We seem to have invested a lot of time and effort, but we still don't have the information we need to improve our processes and make this process 'thing' work."

MAINTAINING MOMENTUM

So, maintaining focus and momentum throughout this transition period is crucial and is likely to require very strong leadership commitment, direction, and engagement from the Process Owner and the Process Leadership Team.

One of the key ways in which the momentum for your Six Sigma Process Management effort can be maintained and further accelerated is through conducting regular *process reviews*.

These meetings will need to be led by the Process Owner, who should also take ownership for scheduling and, ideally, chairing these meetings. Initially, it might be beneficial for the MBB designated to the process to take a facilitation role. In any event, these process review meetings will need to be very carefully planned and executed in order to maximize their impact and effectiveness.

QUICK DEFINITION

Process Reviews are regularly held meetings led by the Process Owner in which the Process Leadership Team reviews process performance and agrees to actions to further improve process performance.

Essentially, the purpose of Process Reviews—we recommend that they be held monthly at a minimum—are to enable the Process Owner and the Process Leadership Team to:

- Review process performance using the *Health of the Process dashboard;*
- Monitor and guide the development of new scorecards and metrics;
- Assess progress on closing data gaps;

- Manage the project portfolio:
  - Identify and prioritize new improvement opportunities
  - Assess progress on improvement plans
  - Conduct project tollgate reviews
  - Implement corrective actions
- Manage the Change communication and Engagement activities such as communicating the process POA, regular updates on process performance, and details of project successes.

You will find the approach that works best for your organization as you get into a routine on these important meetings. For example, depending on your organization's culture and way of doing things, you might wish to add some team-building activities if you feel this would help the team in its formative stages. Ideally, the agenda really should become standardized from meeting to meeting.

In addition, there will be activities that the Process Leadership Team will need to perform with less frequency than the agenda items mentioned above—perhaps quarterly or annually. These include such things as:

- Review progress against the process vision (POA);
- Evaluate process goals and objectives to ensure the performance bar is set high enough;
- Formally align process goals across all *process participants* as part of your regular performance management and planning process;
- Establish appropriate Reward and Recognition mechanisms to drive cross-functional, end-to-end behaviors;
- Invite external customers and other process constituents (suppliers/partners) to participate in an end-to-end Process Review meeting;

Finally, it's very important that the Process Leadership Team doesn't try to manage its process(es) in a vacuum! The Process Owner and members of the Process Leadership Team should be conducting regular meetings with their counterparts who have accountability for other core processes within the organization to ensure alignment across the company's value streams.

Now let's turn our attention to the first of the three key areas that we committed to address in this section.

1. MANAGING A PORTFOLIO OF PROJECTS ACROSS THE END-TO-END PROCESS

One of the key benefits of Six Sigma Process Management is that it enables an end-to-end process perspective of improvement opportunities, whether proposed, in-progress, or completed projects. This enables your organization to focus its improvement efforts on those projects that will generate the largest possible benefits to customers and other key stakeholders of your end-to-end process(es).

QUICK DEFINITION

A project portfolio is the entire listing of projects being managed by the Process Leadership Team.

Without this perspective, it's highly likely that different improvement teams, however well intentioned, will not be sufficiently well aligned and coordinated to tackle the crucial end-to-end process "Y's" in your core processes. Consequently, their efforts will most likely be suboptimized.

So, viewing all of your proposed and active projects as they relate to your core processes—i.e., taking a process-focused project portfolio perspective—is a very important component of successful *process governance*.

There are various ways in which the Process Owner and the Process Leadership Team can review the *project portfolio* as part of their regular *process reviews*. We are going to focus on four key approaches that can be used. In doing so we will show you how you can understand your end-to-end process project portfolio by:

a. Process subprocess
b. Project type and Execution method
c. Ease of Implementation and Value Creation
d. Execution Timeline

Finally in this section we show you how the above perspectives can be brought together into a powerful picture that can be very helpful in managing your project portfolio.

(A) THE SUBPROCESS PERSPECTIVE

A simple approach—that enables the Process Leadership Team to understand which areas of their process they're focusing their improvement efforts on—is to map all of your projects against the subprocesses of your end-to-end process (see Figure 4-2).

This *"mapping"* enables the Process Leadership Team to then ask three very important questions:

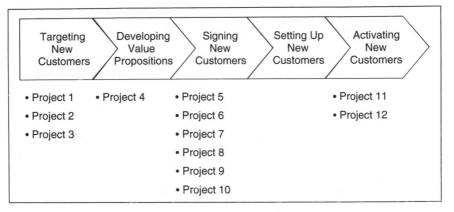

FIGURE 4-2. The subprocess perspective of our example customer acquisition process.

1. "Are we focusing our improvement efforts on those areas of the process where the data is telling us we have problems?" For example, why do we have so many projects focusing on the "Signing New Customers" subprocess when our customer data may be telling us that we have major issues with the "Setting Up New Customers" subprocess? We don't have a single project focusing on this subprocess!

2. "Are there any linkages or overlaps between projects that we need to be aware of?" For example, we might find that the scope of Project 4 overlaps with the way in which Project 6 is currently scoped.

3. "Do we have the capacity to successfully execute these projects in these subprocesses?" For example, do we really have sufficient resources and change capabilities within our organization to simultaneously and successfully execute six projects in the "Signing New Customers" subprocess?

In summary, this perspective creates a very useful picture to spark discussion and further questions about our project portfolio.

(B) THE PROJECT TYPE AND EXECUTION METHOD PERSPECTIVE

We need to recognize that the projects we identify through our Six Sigma Process Management approach will not be the same in terms of their scope, urgency, complexity, and the knowledge required to successfully execute them. Consequently, we can and should utilize different execution methods, tools, and techniques on a situational project basis to maximize the

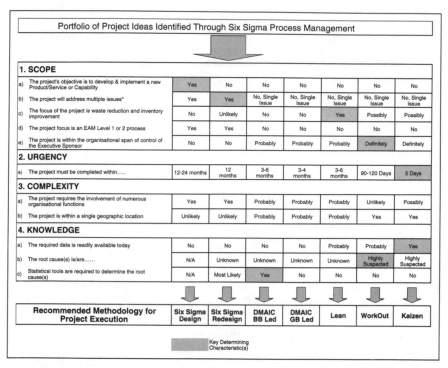

Portfolio of Project Ideas Identified Through Six Sigma Process Management							
1. SCOPE							
a) The project's objective is to develop & implement a new Product/Service or Capability	Yes	No	No	No	No	No	No
b) The project will address multiple issues*	Yes	Yes	No, Single Issue	No, Single Issue	No, Single Issue	No, Single Issue	No, Single Issue
c) The focus of the project is waste reduction and inventory improvement	No	Unlikely	No	No	Yes	Possibly	Possibly
d) The project focus is an EAM Level 1 or 2 process	Yes	Yes	No	No	No	No	No
e) The project is within the organisational span of control of the Executive Sponsor	No	No	Probably	Probably	Probably	Definitely	Definitely
2. URGENCY							
a) The project must be completed within.....	12-24 months	12 months	3-6 months	3-4 months	3-6 months	90-120 Days	5 Days
3. COMPLEXITY							
a) The project requires the involvement of numerous organisational functions	Yes	Yes	Probably	Probably	Probably	Unlikely	Possibly
b) The project is within a single geographic location	Unlikely	Unlikely	Probably	Probably	Probably	Yes	Yes
4. KNOWLEDGE							
a) The required data is readily available today	No	No	No	No	Probably	Probably	Yes
b) The root cause(s) is/are......	N/A	Unknown	Unknown	Unknown	Unknown	Highly Suspected	Highly Suspected
c) Statistical tools are required to determine the root cause(s)	N/A	Most Likely	Yes	No	No	No	No
Recommended Methodology for Project Execution	Six Sigma Design	Six Sigma Redesign	DMAIC BB Led	DMAIC GB Led	Lean	WorkOut	Kaizen

Key Determining Characteristic(s)

FIGURE 4-3. The project type and execution method perspective. © *Roland Cavanagh and Rowland Hayler (Dec. 2004)*

efficiency and effectiveness—do you remember those terms(?)[1]—of our improvement efforts.

In Figure 4-3, we have shown a simple filter that can be used to help you determine the most appropriate execution method, based on the Scope, Urgency, Complexity, and Knowledge characteristics of each project within your portfolio.

Your Process Improvement Teams—with guidance provided by the process designated MBB—should ideally perform this type of assessment prior to each process review meeting.

As with the previous project portfolio perspective, this approach enables the Process Leadership Team to push their thinking and challenge their organization in order to have the best portfolio of projects. For example, if 8 of our 12 projects are major Six Sigma Design projects, how likely is it that we have the required resources and capacity to simultaneously and successfully execute these projects? Probably very low!

The best project portfolios are those that are carefully balanced—containing different types of projects—to mitigate against any adverse risk. It's very rarely a good idea to *"put all of your eggs in one basket!"*

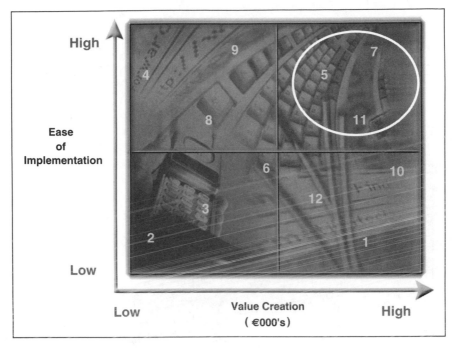

FIGURE 4-4. The ease of implementation and value creation perspective. *Courtesy of Pivotal Resources, Inc.*

(C) THE EASE OF IMPLEMENTATION AND VALUE CREATION PERSPECTIVE

Another approach that the Process Leadership Team can take to review their project portfolio is to create a simple matrix[2] that can be used to plot the projects across the two key dimensions of Ease of Implementation and Value Creation. Other dimensions that are often used with this method are Risk and Return, Value and Complexity, Scale and Difficulty. (See Figure 4-4.)

This perspective can provide a valuable snapshot of your project portfolio and is a good mechanism to effectively prioritize your project opportunities. As with the other portfolio review methods, this approach will also generate a large number of questions and discussion. While value creation should be quantitative, quite often ease of implementation can be highly subjective.

(D) THE EXECUTION TIMELINE PERSPECTIVE

A further perspective that is very important for the Process Leadership Team to have in order to effectively prioritize their project portfolio is a picture of the timeline for the proposed project sequencing—ideally framed within a

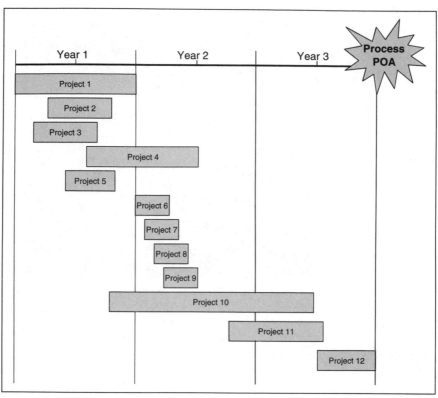

FIGURE 4-5.

multiyear plan (often called a Multigeneration Plan) that shows the planned journey toward the Process POA (Point of Arrival). (See Figure 4-5.)

As with the earlier tools, this provides yet another "snapshot" of the project portfolio that will undoubtedly generate further questions and discussion.

Assembling a Consolidated Picture of Your Project Portfolio

Now that we have developed four different "snapshots" of our end-to-end process project portfolio for the Process Leadership Team, the next logical step is to assemble these "snapshots" into a complete picture (see Figure 4-6).

This consolidated picture of our end-to-end process project portfolio provides a highly useful tool for evaluating, approving, prioritizing, and sequencing improvement efforts across the process. It should be continually updated and reviewed by the Process Leadership Team as a key component of each *process review* meeting.

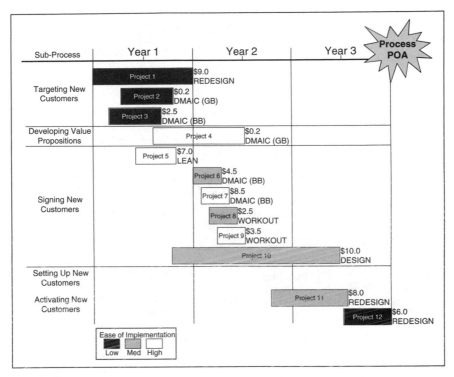

FIGURE 4-6.

Control Basics

In thinking about our Six Sigma Process Management approach within the context of DMAIC, we're now moving into the Control phase.

QUICK DEFINITION

Control: Ensure that sustainable benefits are delivered and the solution is leveraged.

The key components of the Control phase are outlined in Figure 4-7. Going forward, the Process Leadership Team will need to focus a significant amount of their time and effort in ensuring that these components are established as part of their ongoing *process governance* approach.

For now, we're only going to focus on what we consider to be the most crucial component of the Control phase for the Process Leadership Team, and that is Performance Management. Specifically, we'll focus on

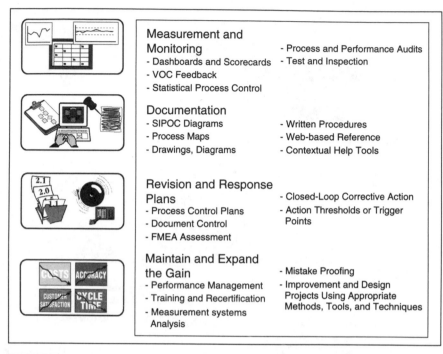

Measurement and Monitoring
- Dashboards and Scorecards
- VOC Feedback
- Statistical Process Control
- Process and Performance Audits
- Test and Inspection

Documentation
- SIPOC Diagrams
- Process Maps
- Drawings, Diagrams
- Written Procedures
- Web-based Reference
- Contextual Help Tools

Revision and Response Plans
- Process Control Plans
- Document Control
- FMEA Assessment
- Closed-Loop Corrective Action
- Action Thresholds or Trigger Points

Maintain and Expand the Gain
- Performance Management
- Training and Recertification
- Measurement systems Analysis
- Mistake Proofing
- Improvement and Design Projects Using Appropriate Methods, Tools, and Techniques

FIGURE 4-7. Key components of the Six Sigma Process Management Control phase. *Courtesy of Pivotal Resources, Inc.*

how the team can use end-to-end process metrics to evaluate performance and what they can do to establish the required cross-functional performance accountabilities and behaviors necessary to achieve improved end-to-end process performance. This, then, is the second key area that we will address.

2. CAREFULLY MEASURING TO SUCCESSFULLY MANAGE—USING PROCESS DASHBOARDS AND SCORECARDS

Data—and more importantly, data translated into meaningful and actionable information—is a crucial requirement for successful *process governance*.

Without the ability to continuously and intelligently measure performance *and* analyze that performance across a comprehensive range of dimensions, you will not be able to manage and continuously optimize your process performance and meet the changing requirements of your customers and other key stakeholders. This is equally true for participants operating in your processes at all levels of the organization—from the Process Owner(s), to your customer-facing frontline employees and associates.

LINKING MEASURES TO SUCCESSFULLY MANAGE

Much has been written about the value of measurement and balanced score-cards. Here's what Philip Green, the CEO of P&O Ned Lloyd, a U.S. $6-Bn. Company, has to say.*

"I am a great believer in the direct correlation in high performing companies between staff, customers and shareholders... At DHL [a former company] we put a lot of effort into measuring what staff and customers thought, understanding the issues and doing something about it . . . If you don't measure something you can't manage it."

The Independent.—Jan 8, 2005, London, UK.

If you already have in place the requirements described in Chapter 3, your Six Sigma Process Management measurement infrastructure is well on the way to being established. However, be aware that while the key VOC, VOB, and VOP data requirements might have now been defined, it's highly likely that your Process Leadership Team will not have access to all of the information that they require immediately.

In our experience, trying to obtain some very fundamental and basic knowledge about your end-to-end process might be highly frustrating. On many occasions we've seen companies really struggle just to get very basic information such as the end-to-end unit cost or cycle time, and in some cases, even total volume throughput. If this is the case with your organization, trying to understand such important things about your process as *Rolled Throughput Yield* and *Process Capability* might not be possible at the moment!

However, as we explored in earlier chapters, at the heart of your Six Sigma Process Management approach is your measurement system—not only what, why, when, where, and how we're going to measure, but also how we're going to efficiently and effectively communicate our process performance throughout the organization, based on process participants' specific data and information needs.

So, one of the initial activities for the Process Owner and the Process Leadership Team, and a crucial step in establishing Performance Management, is to establish a *Health of the Process* dashboard or scorecard that will enable you to regularly monitor the performance of your end-to-end process across a few crucial dimensions. (See Figure 4-8.) It's highly likely that the process designated MBB will need to provide a significant amount of support to ensure that the appropriate measures—perhaps six to eight in total—are identified, that robust operational definitions are documented and agreed, and that the dashboard is visually highly impactful.

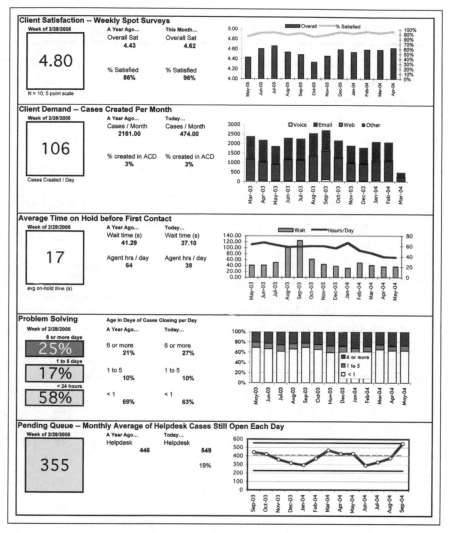

FIGURE 4-8. This Health of the Process Scorecard (Process Dashboard) is from MIT's Information Services & Technology department. Their primary role is to provide services to the MIT campus community. Note the excellent use of graphics and charts. *Reproduced with the kind permission of Rob Smyser, Senior Consultant, Client Support R&D— MIT Information Services & Technology.*

Your *Health of the Process dashboard* is a key tool that should be used at each *process review* meeting to determine performance and progress towards the end-to-end process Point of Arrival (POA).

In addition, from a performance review perspective, the dashboard can be used as the starting point for drilling down into the process to identify where specific defects have occurred.

A clearly defined and carefully constructed measurement hierarchy is required to ensure that performance on each of the key dashboard metrics can be both rolled up, and decomposed throughout all levels of the process.

For example, if the Process Leadership Team reviews their Health of the Process scorecard and identifies poor performance—let's say their cycle time metric is indicating they're failing to meet the cycle time target—their measurement system needs to be constructed in such a way as to enable them to identify which functional areas or external suppliers contributed to this situation. This is the start point in getting the issue(s) scoped and the process performance improved!

Increasingly, companies are using real-time, digitalized approaches to ensure that they have up-to-date process information at their fingertips. Our counsel is always to get the measurement "basics" in place first and then automate. We've seen too many incidents where companies have jumped to an automated approach to measurement before fully considering the what, why, when, where, and how of their measurement approach. They essentially end up with a highly automated (and generally expensive) bad measurement system!

3. ESTABLISHING CROSS-FUNCTIONAL ACCOUNTABILITIES AND BEHAVIORS

The final area that we would like to focus on with regard to *process governance* is the role of the Process Owner and Process Leadership Team in setting cross-functional accountabilities for end-to-end process performance throughout the organization.

REQUIRED LEADERSHIP BEHAVIORS TO ACHIEVE BUSINESS PROCESS LEADERSHIP

- Maniacal focus on meeting the needs of the customer and key stakeholders of the end-to-end process.
- Invests time to actively engage in, and support, cross-functional collaboration and teamwork.
- Prepared to make trade-off decisions between functions to benefit the customer.
- Manages by facts and data.
- Visible, continuous display and communication of cross-functional behaviors.

This is a crucial component of your Six Sigma Process Management approach, without which the required cross-functional behaviors are highly unlikely to materialize. It's also one of the most challenging steps on your journey to business process leadership because the change implications are significant.

Today, many organizations measure and manage process performance function by function, as opposed to across the entire end-to-end process. Similarly today, while many organizations reward and recognize performance based on the results of the overall company—at a personal performance level, it's highly likely that a large part of an employee's reward and recognition package is based on the results achieved by the function (e.g., Finance, Operations, Sales) in which they work.

Such an approach spectacularly fails to focus employees' actions and behaviors on the customers' experiences of the process and perpetuates a functional (silo-ed) focus. In many cases this is at the expense of the customers and other process participants. In our experiences, this situation appears to be endemic in many companies! Perhaps you have witnessed this situation in your own career, perhaps even in your own organization today!

AN ALTERNATE WAY

If your Process Leadership Team is truly serious about achieving business process leadership—and in some cases this could be a very big "*if*"—an alternate approach to managing performance is required.

Let's revisit our Customer Acquisition process for a final time and approach it with Performance Management in mind. Here's another thought-provoking question to consider: "How can we encourage and reward the cross-functional behaviors that are required to achieve business process leadership?" (See Figure 4-9.)

We won't ask you to jot down your answers this time!

In our experience, the key question that needs to be addressed for people in any change situation is "What's in It for Me" (WIIFM). If they don't see a compelling reason to change, they won't. And often they have to see significant benefits, over and above what they current have, to commit

---

Remember:

$$R = Q \times A$$

With little **A**cceptance of our approach, the **Q**uality of our Process Management **R**esults will be severely restricted.

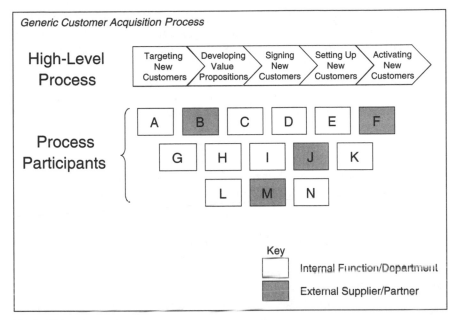

FIGURE 4-9.

to the change. Swapping what I already have for something of the same value isn't really compelling enough!

It's a simple, although at times unsavory, fact that people generally need to be given incentives to demonstrate and adopt new behaviors, and for many people in your organization, cross-functional behaviors will be new.

We've seen a number of organizations who attempt to create these new cross-functional behaviors by changing things around on their organizational charts. For example, these companies would have all of the internal functions (A, C, D, E, G, H, I K, L, and N in the above process schematic, Figure 4-9) reporting into the Process Owner.

While this is one approach that might work from time to time, we would *not* recommend such an approach at this point for the simple reason that the scope of the change required often severely impacts the business—in some cases, bringing it to a complete standstill. What's more—despite any messages that leaders communicate to their organization about the reasons for making such changes (e.g., to achieve a stronger *external* focus), the change process in itself will actually create a very large *internal* focus as people try to figure out the organizational implications—WIIFM!

While it's possible that your Six Sigma Process Management approach *might* necessitate some organizational changes down the road, the best approach that most organizations can take at the start of their Six Sigma Process Management effort is to find subtler ways to create a shared and cross-functional accountability for their end-to-end process performance.

Given the WIIFM mindset, the approach we highly recommend is to use performance-related pay (bonuses!) as a means to initially motivate and instill cross-functional behaviors. A key component that should be used to drive the performance-related pay is the *Health of the Process scorecard*. This approach applies equally to your management of third-party suppliers who participate in the process supply chain. The Health of the Process scorecard should be an integral component of your commercial contract and Service Level Agreement with these partners.

In the example shown below, there are a number of components that are used to determine an individual's performance-related pay. The key difference with the implementation of Six Sigma Process Management is that the individual no longer receives a bonus based upon the performance of their function (e.g., Finance, Operations), but based on the performance of the cross-functional, end-to-end process.

This approach fosters, recognizes, and rewards the cross-functional behaviors that are crucial to achieving business process leadership. We call it the "Three Musketeers" approach—"One for All, and All for One!" In other words, all of the process participants within your end-to-end process either all succeed or fail together, depending on the extent to which the end-to-end process meets its targets (as contained in your Health of the Process scorecard) or not.

There's no better message that the Process Leadership Team can send their respective organizations than committing to such an approach themselves at the very start of their Six Sigma Process Management journey!

SUMMARY

To successfully maximize the performance of your end-to-end core processes on an ongoing basis requires strong *process governance*. This can be particularly challenging because you will need to understand and manage performance from an end-to-end process perspective as opposed to your traditional function-by-function view of the world.

DRIVERS OF PERFORMANCE RELATED PAY:	BEFORE SSPM	WITH SSPM
• Overall Company Performance	20%	20%
• End-to-End Process Performance	0%	40%
• Function Performance	50%	10%
• Individual Performance	30%	30%

One of the key ways in which the momentum for your Six Sigma Process Management effort can be maintained and further accelerated is through conducting regular *process reviews* that enable you to:

1. Manage a portfolio of projects across the end-to-end process;
2. Use process dashboards and scorecards to review performance and make better-informed decisions;
3. Establish and foster cross-functional accountabilities and behaviors.

NOTES

1. Effectiveness can be thought of as the extent to which the *"output"* meets the needs of the customer. Efficiency can be thought of as the quantity of resources required to produce the *"output."* These typically include such things as people, time, money, and materials.
2. Often known as a Filtering Matrix.

WHAT IS THE FUTURE OF SIX SIGMA PROCESS MANAGEMENT?

In this final chapter, we thought that it might be interesting and help ful to offer our perspectives on what a *"future-state"* Six Sigma Process Managed organization might look like. We think of this *snapshot* as a rep- resentation of the highest possible level of *process maturity* that can be achieved—well, for now at least!

We are often asked if any organizations have achieved this level of process maturity. While we are aware of several companies—such as ABB, Cisco, Dell, Glaxo Smith Kline—that have a number of these *process man- agement attributes* in place (perhaps your company could be included in this list as well)—we have yet to find a single company that is able to demon- strate process maturity at the levels we describe on the following pages. If you know of such an organization, please tell us!

We have chosen to include this picture of a *future-state* Six Sigma Process Managed organization for three key reasons:

1. We believe that it's helpful to have an understanding of what we can aspire to. We believe this *picture collage*[1] of a *"future-state"* process- managed organization can provide you with insights and ideas on what might be possible for your own company;

2. As we described in Chapter 2, this *"future-state"* picture can serve as a good benchmark to assess your own organization's current process management maturity. Try asking yourself this question as you review the following attributes: "To what extent do these business *process leadership* components exist in my organization today?"

3. Depending on your answers to the above question, you can identify potential areas that you might need to focus on in order to further strengthen and improve your organization's *process management*

101

ASSESSING PROCESS MATURITY

Dell—whom we consider one of the most mature process-managed organizations today—uses a Maturity Assessment to determine its Business Process Improvement (BPI) Six Sigma maturity. They evaluate their performance on a number of dimensions such as Leadership, Strategic Planning, and Human Resource Management. They characterize their maturity in one of five ways::

1. Novice
2. Awareness
3. Competence
4. Maturity
5. Mastery

A similar approach can be taken to evaluate process maturity.

---

maturity. Hopefully we've given you plenty of ideas on how you might go about this in earlier chapters!

There are various ways in which we could have *"framed"* our *"future-state"* picture. We decided to use the three key themes of Process Leadership, Process Knowledge, and Process Execution. In our view, organizations need to excel at all three to achieve sustainable process performance and superior business results.

Here's how we can link these three key themes together in a way that continually informs, shapes, and drives process maturity (see Figure 5-1). The following sections look at our future-state picture.

THE HIGHEST LEVEL OF SIX SIGMA PROCESS MANAGEMENT MATURITY

Imagine an organization where the following operational characteristics are the *"way of life."* Is this the Six Sigma Process Management aspiration for your company? We strongly believe that in the future, the world's leading process-managed organizations will demonstrate many, if not all, of the operational characteristics described below:

1. PROCESS LEADERSHIP
    a. A PROCESS-LED ORGANIZATION
        *   A senior leader has been appointed as a Process Owner for each of the company's core end-to-end processes. All sen-

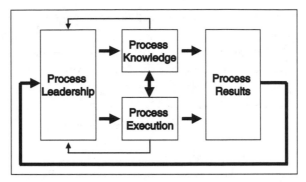

FIGURE 5-1.

ior leader are equipped with the knowledge, skills, and resources to be highly successful in this role;

- Each Process Owner leads a Process Leadership Team consisting of leaders who represent each operational function, support function, and external third party involved in the end-to-end core process;

- The Process Leadership Team (chaired by the Process Owner) meets monthly at a minimum to conduct a data-based review of end-to-end process performance, identify issues, review existing improvement projects, identify additional improvement priorities, and launch new projects;

- The Process Leadership Team regularly meets with and listens to customers—existing, prospective, and lost, end-to-end process participants, especially frontline customer-facing employees; and third-party suppliers;

- The Process Leadership Team continually fosters a key stakeholder-driven end-to-end process culture that transcends all functional boundaries;

- The Process Leadership Team deploys resources within an end-to-end process context. E.g., MBB's, Lean Masters, and Kaizen experts are dedicated to each core process.

b. AN INTEGRATED PROCESS VISION

- A customer and key-stakeholder-defined Process POA based on known process excellence and competitive benchmarking, fully aligned with the long-term strategic objectives of the company, has been developed for each end-to-end core process;

- The relationships, linkages, and interdependencies between each end-to-end core process are fully understood;

- Each Process POA has been translated into meaningful, measurable, and aligned goals for each process participant

(internal and external third party) engaged in the end-to-end
process;

- A multigenerational plan has been developed and is regularly updated to guide the organization's journey towards
each of its Process POAs.

c. AN END-TO-END PROCESS RESULTS ORIENTATION

- Cross-functional, end-to-end core-process-oriented reward
and recognition systems are in place. E.g., process participants are rewarded on end-to-end process performance.
Only a relatively small percentage of their compensation is
driven by the performance of their own functional unit;

- The Health of the Process (HotP) scorecard—focusing on
end-to-end process performance—drives all reward and
recognition mechanisms;

- Performance and results are communicated to the organization using the Health of the Process scorecard.

**d. AN END-TO-END PROCESS-ORIENTED APPROACH
TO DECISION MAKING**

- Decisions are made using a consolidated end-to-end
process portfolio approach to maximize value creation:
  - Investment and trade-off decisions are made across
  the end-to-end process;
  - Project selection is made within the context of the end-
  to-end process, based upon what will have the greatest
  impact on ultimate value creation;
  - Human resource selection, development, and succession
  planning decisions are taken within the context of the
  end-to-end process.
- All decisions are made using data based facts.

e. PROCESS CAPABILITIES BUILDING

- Career progression is dependent upon demonstrable
(1) process improvement success using Lean Six Sigma techniques and (2) cross-functional leadership behaviors. Clearly
defined career progression paths exist within the end-to-end
process. E.g., Green Belt to Black Belt to Master Black Belt
to Lead Master Black Belt to Deployment Champion to
Process Leader to Process Owner;

- All process participants have received appropriate levels of
Lean Six Sigma training;

- There is a continuous investment commitment (time and
resources) to researching, identifying, and integrating

leading-edge approaches to further expand process capabilities and maturity.

    f. COMMUNICATION

- A commonly held view exists at all levels of the process organization (end-to-end, top to bottom) about the Process POA, how it's going to be achieved, where the organization is on the journey, and what the next set of immediate priorities are;

- All employees understand the Process structure, the various processes' roles, and where and how they fit in the process-based organization.

- Regular communication is provided by the Process Owner and Process Leadership Team to process participants on progress towards the Process POA—including performance results and successes, project updates, challenges, and opportunities.

2. PROCESS KNOWLEDGE

    a. A BALANCED SET OF END-TO-END PROCESS MEASUREMENTS

- A comprehensive, sophisticated, and diverse array of customer and process listening mechanisms are in place;

- A balanced health of the process scorecard is used for each core process to determine end-to-end process performance and progress against the Process POA;

- The balanced scorecard for each core process uses leading and lagging indicators that are empirically linked to the ultimate drivers of Customer behavior for that process;

- The balanced scorecard for each core process breaks down into a hierarchy of measures that are seamlessly linked across, and up and down, the end-to-end process to facilitate performance management and problem solving;

- Operational Definitions have been established for each measure and are commonly understood and used across the entire end-to-end process;

- A balanced set of KPI's are built in from the start of any new initiative;

- All measurements are continually reviewed and assessed to ensure that the leading process indicators are correct.

    b. A ROBUST MEASUREMENT ENGINE

- An executive information system is in place for the Process Owner and the Process Leadership Team;

- All end-to-end process performance measurement is fully automated with digitized real-time performance reporting available as required by each process participant;
- In-process feedback mechanisms alert process participants of any in-process defects prior to receipt by the customer;
- The visual display of process data facilitates the quick and easy identification of any out-of-control activities or performance;
- All end-to-end process documentation is held on a dynamic, easily accessible database with the appropriate change controls built in;
- Measurements are continually refined and strengthened to ensure an up-to-date data-driven understanding of core process performance.

3. PROCESS EXECUTION
   a. DAILY OPERATIONS
   - The end-to-end process environment is founded upon Lean Six Sigma and other leading principles, methods, tools, and techniques;
   - New products and services are brought to market with full knowledge of process capability and process performance measures;
   - Process performance measurement, benchmarking, improvement, and management are the "way of life;"
   - An automated change management process is in place to ensure that all process stakeholders review, challenge, and approve process changes before they're implemented;
   - Process participants continually strive to mistake-proof their process, making it impossible to do is wrong;
   - The end-to-end process environment is engendered with a continuous quest for improvement at all levels of the organization.

   b. A CONTINUOUS QUEST FOR IMPROVEMENT
   - Lean Six Sigma and other leading techniques are appropriately and continuously employed to minimize in-process waste, optimize inventory performance, and eliminate defects;
   - There is extensive engagement of frontline and middle managers on project selection;
   - Process participants are encouraged and empowered to continuously look for ways to improve the end-to-end process;

- Kaizen events are used to showcase and implement employee suggestions;
- Best practices are well documented and easily accessible to facilitate the transfer of best practices;
- The leverage of solutions, knowledge, and best practices is evident and rewarded;

c. PROCESS LANGUAGE, METHODS, TOOLS AND TECHNIQUES

- Common process management and improvement vocabulary, methods, tools, and techniques are in place and appropriately used.

It's possible that the above list of characteristics isn't complete. We're quite sure that others will identify some additional *"future-state"* characteristics that we haven't yet identified.

The point, however, is that for many companies, achieving the degree of process maturity described above will be a significant multiyear effort in itself!

FINAL NOTE

As we explained early on—one of *our* key measures of success for this book is to simply encourage you to think differently about *business process leadership*, ask questions, and open further discussions within your own organization on what business process leadership means and how it can be achieved.

Consequently, we have intentionally covered a number of topics in this book:

- We have defined Six Sigma Process Management and explained why it's important in achieving Business Process Leadership. We have also described how it can help your organization achieve improved *process maturity* and operational performance;
- We have introduced the change leadership requirements that we believe are crucial to successfully implementing a Six Sigma Process Management approach;
- We have offered a step-by-step methodology for implementing a *process management system* within the context of the Lean Six Sigma DMAIC framework. We have also outlined the key tools required to establish the Six Sigma Process Management system;

- We have focused on the Six Sigma Process Management governance requirements that we believe are crucial for successfully managing your *end-to-end processes* on an ongoing basis—and finally;

- We have explored the future of process management and outlined many of the key characteristics of a *"future-state"* organization that has successfully embedded Six Sigma Process Management into its business operations.

We certainly don't pretend to have all of the answers, but we very much hope that our comments, ideas, and insights have provided you with some new perspectives and suggestions on what Six Sigma Process Management is all about—and how it can enable your organization to achieve significantly improved *business process leadership*.

We wish you every success on your journey!

For additional information on SSPM please write to mailto:info@sspm-ideas.com

NOTES

1. We use the term *"collage"* because we've assembled this *"picture"* from numerous *"sources."*

RECOMMENDED READING

While there are many good references available on Six Sigma and Lean, we have chosen only a few that we believe are most relevant to assist with your Process Management journey.

SIX SIGMA LEADERSHIP

Beecroft, Dennis G., Grace L. Duffy, and John W. Moran. *The Executive Guide to Improvement and Change*. ASQ, 2003.

Pande, Peter S., Robert P. Neuman, and Roland R. Cavanagh. *The Six Sigma Way*. New York: McGraw Hill, 2000.

Watson, Gregory H. *Six Sigma for Business Leaders*. Goal QPC, 2004.

SIX SIGMA REFERENCE

Pande, Peter, and Larry Holpp. *What is Six Sigma?* New York: McGraw Hill, 2002.

Pande, Peter S., Neuman, Robert P., and Cavanagh, Roland R. *The Six Sigma Way Team Fieldbook: An Implementation Guide for Process Improvement Teams*. New York: McGraw Hill, 2002.

Pyzdek, Thomas. *The Six Sigma Handbook, Revised and Expanded*. New York: Mcgraw Hill, 2003.

CUSTOMER

Gale, Bradley T. *Managing Customer Value*. Free Press, 1994.

Lawton, Robin L. *Creating a Customer-Centered Culture*. ASQ, 1993.

PROCESS MANAGEMENT

Harrington, H. James. *Business Process Improvement*. New York: McGraw Hill, 1991.

BENCHMARKING

Camp, Robert C. *Benchmarking*. ASQC Quality Press, 1989.

LEAN

Womack, James P. and Jones, Daniel T. *Lean Thinking*. New York: Simon & Schuster, 1996.